ACT
ASSESSMENT®
MATH

flash

MARK N. WEINFELD

PETERSON'S

THOMSON LEARNING™

Australia • Canada • Mexico • Singapore • Spain • United Kingdom • United States

PETERSON'S

THOMSON LEARNING

About Peterson's

Founded in 1966, Peterson's, a division of Thomson Learning, is the nation's largest and most respected provider of lifelong learning online resources, software, reference guides, and books. The Education Supersite^{SM} at petersons.com—the Web's most heavily traveled education resource—has searchable databases and interactive tools for contacting U.S.-accredited institutions and programs. CollegeQuest® (CollegeQuest.com) offers a complete solution for every step of the college decision-making process. GradAdvantage^{TM} (GradAdvantage.org), developed with Educational Testing Service, is the only electronic admissions service capable of sending official graduate test score reports with a candidate's online application. Peterson's serves more than 55 million education consumers annually.

Thomson Learning is among the world's leading providers of lifelong learning, serving the needs of individuals, learning institutions, and corporations with products and services for both traditional classrooms and for online learning. For more information about the products and services offered by Thomson Learning, please visit www.thomsonlearning.com. Headquartered in Stamford, Connecticut, with offices worldwide, Thomson Learning is part of The Thomson Corporation (www.thomson.com), a leading e-information and solutions company in the business, professional, and education marketplaces. The Corporation's common shares are listed on the Toronto and London stock exchanges.

An American BookWorks Corporation Project

For more information, contact Peterson's, 2000 Lenox Drive, Lawrenceville, NJ 08648; 800-338-3282; or find us on the World Wide Web at: www.petersons.com/about

Library of Congress Cataloging-in-Publication Data

Weinfeld, Mark.
    Peterson's ACT math flash : the quick and easy way to learn problem-solving skills / Mark Weinfeld.
        p.   cm.
    ISBN 0-7689-0628-8
    1. Mathematica—Examinations, questions, etc. 2. ACT Assessment—Study guides.
I. Title.
QA43.W375   1997
510'.76—dc21   97-12094
                                                                                CIP

Printed in Canada

10 9 8 7 6 5 4 3 2 1   03 02 01

CONTENTS

ABOUT ACT MATH FLASH

You're getting ready to take the ACT exam, and you need some last-minute practice. It's a well-known fact that the more practice you have taking models of the actual ACT, the better you will do on the ACT itself. Thus, here's a way to review the mathematics portion of the ACT in a flash.

The questions in ACT Math Flash are the same type of ACT questions that you will find on the test. We have varied the difficulty of the questions so that you will develop a "feel" for the test. Furthermore, every question is analyzed. We have provided the mathematical *concepts* behind the questions, stated the *formulas*, where appropriate, given *definitions*, and finally, we have given you complete step-by-step *solutions* to every problem.

Using ACT Math Flash

1. **Format** Notice how the book is set up—each page contains one or two problems, and the solutions follow immediately on the next page. First, answer both questions on the page, fill in your answer blanks, and then check the right answer on the following page. If you have a wrong answer, read through the answer carefully to analyze where you made your mistake. Did you not understand the concept? Was there a calculation error? Was there a formula that you didn't know?

    Make a note where you made your error and then apply it to similar questions you will encounter. Memorize theorems or definitions. Analyze the step-by-step solution process.

2. **Study Strategy** Complete all of the questions. Even if you think a problem is easy, do it anyway. You never know what might be lurking behind a seemingly innocent problem. Take a stab at the difficult problems. Remember, this is only practice, not the real thing.

3. **Analyze the Answer Choices** Remember that these are multiple-choice questions, which means there is only one correct answer. There is often one other answer that may seem correct, but it is

not. For example, with a *slight miscalculation*, you might select the number 5 instead of the number 0.5. All it takes is a decimal point in the wrong place.

The other wrong choices are often solutions that were derived by using the wrong formula or calculation. Test developers know that students often confuse formulas, and they anticipate that by giving you an answer that you might obtain by using the wrong formula. Check the solutions carefully. This is where you will *learn* the material that you don't already know.

The ACT Mathematics Test—And What To Expect!

By the time you are ready to take the ACT you have, hopefully, already learned the material that will be covered on the exam. The topics on this test are taken from ninth through eleventh grade mathematics and covers everything from Pre-Algebra through Trigonometry. Following is the breakdown of the test.

Content	Number of items	Percentage of mathematics test
Pre-Algebra	14	23%
Elementary Algebra	10	17%
Intermediate Algebra	9	15%
Coordinate Geometry	9	15%
Plane Geometry	14	23%
Trigonometry	4	7%
Total	60	100%

This chart should help you focus immediately. How are your skills in Pre-Algebra and Plane Geometry? These are the two areas with the most questions. There are sixty questions on the math exam, and more than half of the exam is Algebra. Learn to spend your time wisely.

The best advice is to use this book and keep practicing and studying.

Good luck!

TEST
1

This test consists of sixty questions and five possible answer choices for each. For each problem, select the answer choice that represents the best solution and shade the corresponding oval.

Note: Unless otherwise stated, all of the following should be assumed:

1. Illustrative figures are NOT necessarily drawn to scale.

2. Geometric figures lie on a plane.

3. The word *line* indicates a straight line.

4. The word *average* indicates arithmetic mean.

1. Which of the following numbers is both a factor of 72 and a multiple of 4?

   8 9

   (A) 2
   (B) 12
   (C) 16
   (D) 18
   (E) 32

2. 17% of 325 is how much more than 7% of 325?

   (A) 3.25
   (B) 6.5
   (C) 32.5
   (D) 48.5
   (E) 65

   55.25

---

1. (A) (B) (C) (D) (E)

2. (A) (B) (C) (D) (E)

 DO YOUR FIGURING HERE

Answer #1:   Ⓑ

Concepts: • Factoring
• Arithmetic

The multiples of 4 are the numbers 4, 8, 12, 16, 20, 24, 28, 32 . . . . Thus, the answer must be either B, C, or E. The factors of 72 are the numbers that divide evenly into 72. Of 12, 16, and 18, only 12 is a factor of 72.

Answer #2:   Ⓒ

Concept: • Computations with percents

This problem can be solved by computing 17% of 325 and 7% of 325 and then subtracting. Since, for example, 17% = 0.17, 17% of 325 = 0.17 × 325 = 55.25, and 7% of 325 = 0.07 × 325 = 22.75. Finally, 55.25 − 22.75 = 32.5.

A much quicker way to do the problem is to note that the difference between 17% of 325 and 7% of 325 is simply 10% of 325, and 10% of 325 is 32.5.

3. If $3^n = 81$, then $n^3 =$

(A) 9
(B) 27
(C) 32
(D) 64
(E) 125

4. $(x^2 + y^2)^2 - (2xy)^2 =$

(A) $(x^2 - y^2)^2$
(B) $(x^2 + y^2)$
(C) $x^2 - y^2$
(D) $2xy$
(E) $4xy$

3. (A) (B) (C) (D) (E)

4. (A) (B) (C) (D) (E)

 DO YOUR FIGURING HERE

$$3n = \frac{81}{3}$$

$$n = 27$$

$$3^n$$

$$\sqrt{x^4 + y^4 - 4x^2y^2}$$

$$(x^2 - y^2)(x^2 - y^2)$$

$$x^2 + y^2 - 2xy$$

Answer #3: (D)

Concept: • Exponential equations

To solve this problem, you must begin by solving the equation $3^n = 81$. An equation that has its variable as an exponent is very difficult to solve unless the numbers are chosen so as to come out "nicely." On the ACT, whenever you see an equation with variable exponents, it will, in fact, always have a "nice" answer. In this case, very simply, $n = 4$, since $3^4 = 81$. Then, $n^3 = 4^3 = 64$.

Answer #4: (A)

Formulas: • $(a + b)^2 = a^2 + 2ab + b^2$
                 • $(a - b)^2 = a^2 - 2ab + b^2$

Concepts: • Binomial products
                 • Algebraic factoring

The straightforward way to do this problem is to simply multiply and then factor the given expression. Thus, using the first formula above,

$$(x^2 + y^2)^2 - (2xy)^2 = (x^4 + 2x^2y^2 + y^4) - 4x^2y^2$$
$$= x^4 + 2x^2y^2 - 4x^2y^2 + y^4 = x^4 - 2x^2y^2 + y^4$$

Then, by the second formula, $x^4 - 2x^2y^2 + y^4 = (x^2 - y^2)^2$.

If you are not sure how to do a problem such as the one above, sometimes you can figure out what the answer has to be by substituting values. For example, if you let $x = 2$ and $y = 1$, the expression $(x^2 + y^2)^2 - (2xy)^2$ becomes $(2^2 + 1^2)^2 - (2(2)(1))^2 = 5^2 - 4^2 = 24 - 16 = 9$.

Now, plug $x = 2$ and $y = 1$ into the answer choices, and look for one that becomes equal to 9. In choice A, $(2^2 - 1^2)^2 = (4 - 1)^2 = 3^2 = 9$. None of the other choices equal 9, so A must be the solution. If, in using this technique, you had, in fact, ended up with two solutions that evaluated out to 9, it would be necessary to try again with different values for x and y.

5. If $3x + 1 = 28$ and $y = x^2$, then $y =$

(A) -3
(B) 3
(C) 9
(D) 27
(E) 81

6. The number of employees at a certain company decreased by 12 in January, increased by 8 in February, and decreased by 5 in March. If the number of employees before these changes was N, then the number of employees after these changes was

(A) $N - 25$
(B) $N - 9$
(C) $N - 1$
(D) $N + 1$
(E) $N + 25$

---

5. Ⓐ Ⓑ Ⓒ Ⓓ ●

6. Ⓐ ● Ⓒ Ⓓ Ⓔ

 DO YOUR FIGURING HERE

$3x + 1 = 28$
$+1 \quad -1$
$y = x^2$
$3x = 27$
$x = 9$
$y = 81$

Answer #5:   Ⓔ

Definition: • Exponents
Concept: • Solving first degree equations

This problem really consists of two smaller problems. You must begin by solving the equation $3x + 1 = 28$ for x, and then use the value you obtain to evaluate y.

To begin: $3x + 1 = 28$ Thus,

$3x = 27$ And

$x = 9$

Now, we must evaluate $y = x^2$, where $x = 9$. Clearly, $y = x^2 = 9^2 = 81$.

Answer #6:   Ⓑ

Concept: • Algebraic notation

The easiest way to do this problem is to simply begin with N, and keep a running total of the changes in the number of employees.

At the end of January, there were N − 12 employees; at the end of February, there were N − 12 + 8 = N − 4 employees; finally, at the end of March, there were N − 4 − 5 = N − 9.

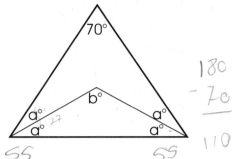

180
- 70
———
110

7. In the triangle above, what is
   the value of *b*?

   (A) 55°
   (B) 70°
   (C) 110°
   (D) 125°
   (E) 140°

---

7. (A)   (B)   (C)   (D)   (E)

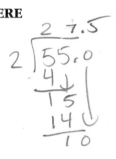 **DO YOUR FIGURING HERE**

Answer #7:   Ⓓ

Concept: • 180° in a triangle
Formula: • In triangle ABC, $a + b + c = 180$

Solving this problem simply requires repetition of the fundamental fact that every triangle contains 180°. First of all, consider the larger triangle. It contains three angles, one of which is 70°, and the other two of which are $a° + a° = 2a°$. Knowing this, we can solve for a.

$$70 + 2a + 2a = 180$$

$$4a = 110$$

$$a = 27\frac{1}{2}$$

Now, look at the smaller triangle. It contains three angles, two of which are $a° = 27\frac{1}{2}°$, and one of which is $b°$. Now, we can solve for b.

$$27\frac{1}{2} + 27\frac{1}{2} + b = 180$$

$$55 + b = 180$$

$$b = 125°$$

8. If $|5x - 2| = 13$, then $x = ?$

(A) 3
(B) −3
(C) −1⅕
(D) − 3 and 1⅕
(E) 3 and −1⅕

9. Which of the following ordered pairs satisfies the equation $2x + 5y = 21$?

(A) (−2, 5)
(B) (2, −5)
(C) (1, 4)
(D) (−1, 5)
(E) (5, −2)

8. Ⓐ Ⓑ Ⓒ Ⓓ ⬤

9. ⬤ Ⓑ Ⓒ Ⓓ Ⓔ

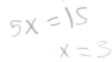

 DO YOUR FIGURING HERE

$$5x = 15$$
$$x = 3$$

$$|5x - 2| = 13$$

$$2(-2) + 25$$

$$5x - 2 = 13$$
$$+2 \quad +2$$

$$5x - 2 = -13$$
$$+2 \quad +2$$

Answer #8:   Ⓔ

Concept: • Solving absolute value equations

It is easy to see that $x = 3$ solves the equation, since $|5(3) - 2| = |15 - 2| = |13| = 13$. Many people, therefore, answer A, and get the question wrong. Absolute value equations typically have two solutions. Of course, the value of x that makes $5x - 2 = 13$ solves the equation, but the value of x that makes $5x - 2 = -13$ also solves the equation, since $|-13| = 13$. Thus, to find the second solution, you must solve the equation $5x - 2 = -13$. The solution of this equation is $x = -1\frac{1}{5}$.

Answer #9:   Ⓐ

Definition: • Ordered pair
Concept: • Solving first-degree equations in one unknown

Since the given equation is a first-degree equation with two unknowns, it has an infinite number of solutions. Thus, there is really no way to find the answer to this problem directly, and the best way to proceed is to simply take the answer choices and try them one at a time until you find the correct one.

For choice A: $2x + 5y = 2(-2) + 5(5) = -4 + 25 = 21$. We were lucky that the first answer we tried was correct; had choice A ended up equaling something other than 21, we would have had to try the other choices.

10. Which of the following is equivalent to $\dfrac{(1 + \tan^2 x)}{\tan^2 x}$?

(A) $\sin^2 x$

(B) $\dfrac{1}{\sin x}$

(C) $\sin x$

(D) $1 + \sin^2 x$

(E) $\dfrac{1}{\sin^2 x}$

$$\frac{1 + \tan^2 x}{\tan^2 x}$$

10. Ⓐ Ⓑ Ⓒ Ⓓ Ⓔ

 DO YOUR FIGURING HERE

$$\frac{\sin^2\theta + \cos^2\theta = 1}{\cos^2\theta} \quad \frac{}{\cos^2\theta} \quad \frac{}{\cos^2\theta}$$

$$\tan^2\theta + 1 = \sec^2\theta$$

$$\frac{\sin^2 + \cos^2 = 1}{\cos 2}$$

$$\frac{\sin^2 + 1}{\cos 2} = \frac{1}{\cos^2}$$

Answer #10: Ⓔ

Concept: • Solving trigonometric identities

Formula: • $1 + \tan^2 x = \sec^2 x$, $\sec x = \dfrac{1}{\cos x}$ and $\tan x = \dfrac{\sin x}{\cos x}$

Definition: • Tangent, secant, sine, cosine

Solving this problem simply requires the application of several of the fundamental trigonometric identities. First of all, recall that $1 + \tan^2 x = \sec^2 x$. Thus,

$$\frac{(1 + \tan^2 x)}{\tan^2 x} = \frac{\sec^2 x}{\tan^2 x}$$

Now, use the fact that $\sec x = \dfrac{1}{\cos x}$ and $\tan x = \dfrac{\sin x}{\cos x}$ to obtain

$$\frac{\sec^2 x}{\tan^2 x} = \frac{\left(\dfrac{1}{\cos^2 x}\right)}{\left(\dfrac{\sin^2 x}{\cos^2 x}\right)} = \left(\frac{1}{\cos^2 x}\right)\left(\frac{\cos^2 x}{\sin^2 x}\right) = \frac{1}{\sin^2 x}.$$

11. What is the slope of the line graphed below?

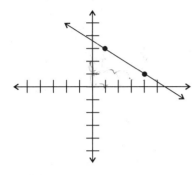

(A) ⅔

(B) ³⁄₂

(C) ⁻³⁄₂

(D) ⁻⅔

(E) ⁻²⁄₅

11. (A) (B) (C) (D) (E)

 DO YOUR FIGURING HERE

Answer #11: ⓓ

Concept: • Slope of a line

Formula: • Slope $= \dfrac{(y_2 - y_1)}{(x_2 - x_1)}$

Since the graph gives the coordinates of two of the points on the line, we simply need to use the formula for the slope of a line to compute the slope. Recall that if (x_1, y_1) and (x_2, y_2) are two points on a line, then the slope is given by

$$\text{slope} = \frac{(y_2 - y_1)}{(x_2 - x_1)}$$

For the two given points, (4, 1) and (1, 3), the slope is

$$\text{slope} = \frac{(y_2 - y_1)}{(x_2 - x_1)} = \frac{(3 - 1)}{(1 - 4)} = \frac{-2}{3}$$

12. Which of the following is true for two parallel lines?

(A) The lines both have a slope of 0.

(B) The lines both have undefined slopes.

(C) The slopes of the two lines are negative reciprocals.

(D) The slopes of the two lines are reciprocals.

(E) The slopes of the two lines are the same.

13. What is the y-intercept of the line $y = \left(-\dfrac{5}{2}\right)x + 4$?

(A) -4

(B) $-\dfrac{5}{2}$

(C) $-\dfrac{5}{8}$

(D) -10

(E) 4

---

12. Ⓐ Ⓑ Ⓒ Ⓓ Ⓔ

13. Ⓐ Ⓑ Ⓒ Ⓓ Ⓔ

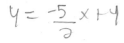

$y = \dfrac{-5}{2}x + 4$

 DO YOUR FIGURING HERE

Answer #12: Ⓔ

Concept:	• Slopes of parallel and perpendicular lines
Formulas:	• If l_1 and l_2 are parallel lines, they have the same slope
	• If l_1 and l_2 are perpendicular lines, their slopes are negative reciprocals

Answering this question simply hinges upon your knowledge of a fundamental (and obvious) fact about parallel lines: a pair of parallel lines have the same steepness, that is to say, the same slope. Thus, the answer is E. For future reference, note that choice C describes two perpendicular lines, and that horizontal lines have a slope of 0, while vertical lines have an undefined slope.

Answer #13: Ⓔ

Concept:	• y-intercept
Formula:	• $y = mx + b$ (The slope-intercept form of a line)

The y-intercept of a line is the y-coordinate of the point where the line crosses the y axis; that is to say, the value of y when x equals 0. There are two ways to answer this question. One is to simply plug $x = 0$ into the given equation of the line. This yields $y = (-\frac{5}{2})x + 4 = (-\frac{5}{2})(0) + 4 = 4$ as the y-intercept. Or, you could just notice that the line is given in the "slope-intercept" form. Just looking at the equation is enough to tell you that the slope of the line is $-\frac{5}{2}$, and the y-intercept is 4.

14. What is the center and the radius of the circle described by the equation:

$(x - 4)^2 + (y + 2)^2 = 25$?

(A) Center $(-4, 2)$, Radius 5
(B) Center $(4, -2)$, Radius 5
(C) Center $(-4, 2)$, Radius 25
(D) Center $(4, -2)$, Radius 25
(E) Center $(2, -4)$, Radius 5

14. Ⓐ Ⓑ Ⓒ Ⓓ Ⓔ

 DO YOUR FIGURING HERE

$(x-4)(x-4) + (y+2)(y+2) = 25$

$x^2 - 8x + 16 + y^2 + 4y + 4 = 25$

$x^2 +$

Answer #14: Ⓑ

Concept: • The equation of a circle

Formula: • $(x - h)^2 + (y - k)^2 = r^2$ represents a circle with center (h, k) and radius r.

You can read the answer to this problem almost directly from the given equation, if you can remember the general form for the equation of a circle:

The equation $(x - h)^2 + (y - k)^2 = r^2$ represents a circle with center (h, k) and radius r.

Now, visualize the equation we have been given rewritten in the equivalent form

$$(x - 4)^2 + (y - (-2))^2 = 5^2$$

and you can see that the center is (4, −2) and the radius is 5.

15. The owner of a convention center placed an order for 25 overhead projectors. The cost for each of the first 15 projectors was $165. Each additional projector ordered cost only $135. What was the total cost of the 25 projectors?

(A) $1,350
(B) $2,610
(C) $3,375
(D) $3,825
(E) $4,125

16. At the beginning of the week, AMPEX stock was selling at 38¼. During the week, the stock declined by 6⅝. What was the price of the stock at the end of the week?

(A) 31⅜
(B) 31⅝
(C) 32⅜
(D) 32½
(E) 32⅝

---

15. (A) (B) (C) (D) (E)

16. (A) (B) (C) (D) (E)

0625

2475
1350

25

🖎 DO YOUR FIGURING HERE

Answer #15: ⒟

Concept: • Arithmetic
Formula: • Cost = unit price × number purchased

This is a very easy question, just requiring you to perform a few multiplications and an addition. The only way to go wrong is to rush and read the problem incorrectly, so simply be careful.

Each of the first 15 projectors costs $165, for a total of 15 × $165 = $2,475

Each of the next 10 projectors costs $135, for a total of 10 × $135 = $1,350

Thus, all 25 projectors cost $2,475 + $1,350 = $3,825.

Answer #16: ⒝

Concept: • Subtraction of fractions

This question just asks you to subtract mixed numbers. Since the closing price of the stock is the original price less the amount of the decline,

Closing Price = $38\frac{1}{4}$ − $6\frac{5}{8}$ = $38\frac{2}{8}$ − $6\frac{5}{8}$.

To perform this subtraction, we must first rewrite $38\frac{2}{8}$ as $37\frac{10}{8}$ (this is what they called "borrowing" in grade school). Then,

$37\frac{10}{8}$ − $6\frac{5}{8}$ = $31\frac{5}{8}$.

17. Which of the following
fractions is the largest?

(A) ¾
(B) ⅞
(C) 9/11
(D) 8/9
(E) ⅘

18. A secretary is paid time and
a half for working overtime.
Last week, he earned $297
for working 9 hours of
overtime. What is his regular
hourly salary?

(A) $9   33
(B) $11
(C) $18
(D) $22
(E) $33

17. Ⓐ Ⓑ Ⓒ Ⓓ Ⓔ

18. Ⓐ Ⓑ Ⓒ Ⓓ Ⓔ

297

9 hrs.

 DO YOUR FIGURING HERE

Answer #17: Ⓓ

Concept: • Writing fractions as decimals

Formula: • To write a/b as a decimal, divide b into a

There are a number of ways to solve this question. One reliable method is to merely rewrite all of the fractions as decimals, from which it would be easy to determine the largest. This process can be sped up by first eliminating the fractions that are clearly not the largest. For example, $3/4$ is out, since all of the other fractions are clearly larger. Similarly, we can eliminate $4/5$ and $7/8$ since $8/9$ is larger than both. This can be seen intuitively; for example, consider two pies, one cut into 8 pieces and one cut into 9. Surely having 7 pieces from the first pie does not give you as much pie as would having 8 pieces from the pie cut into 9 pieces. Thus, the problem reduces into an effort to determine the larger of $8/9$ and $9/11$.

By division, determine that $8/9 \approx .88$, while $9/11 \approx .82$. Thus, $8/9$ is the largest.

Answer #18: Ⓓ

Formula: • Time worked × hourly salary = total salary

The easiest way to proceed is to first determine how much the secretary made during each of the nine overtime hours worked. Since $297/9 = 33$, the secretary made $33 an hour working overtime, in other words, $33 represents $1\frac{1}{2}$ times his regular salary. A little algebra finishes the problem. Let S represent his regular salary. Then,

$(3/2)\ S = 33$ Or, multiplying both sides of the equation by $2/3$,

$S = 33\ (2/3) = 22.$

19. What is the freight charge
for transporting seven drums
of motor oil weighing 165
pounds each, if the charge is
50 cents per pound?

   (A) $82.50
   (B) $265.13
   (C) $484.80
   (D) $577.50
   (E) $787.50

19.

 DO YOUR FIGURING HERE

Answer #19: Ⓓ

Concept: • Arithmetic

Formula: • Cost per pound × number of pounds = total cost

Solving this problem simply means keeping track of what is going on in it. To start, notice that the first thing we need to know is the total number of pounds being shipped, which is determined by multiplying 7 × 165 = 1,155 pounds. Now, each one of these pounds costs 50 cents to ship, so next we multiply 1,155 × 50 cents. Since the answer choices are expressed in dollars, express 50 cents as 0.5 dollars. Then, 1,155 × 0.5 = $577.50.

20. If $A = B(x + C) - Dx$, what is x equal to, in terms of A, B, C, and D?

(A) $\dfrac{(A - BC)}{(B - D)}$

(B) $\dfrac{(A - BC)}{(D - B)}$

(C) $\dfrac{(A + D)}{(B + C)}$

(D) $\dfrac{(A - D)}{(B - C)}$

(E) $\dfrac{(BC - A)}{(B + D)}$

21. A used fax machine is purchased for \$225. This was 45% of the machine's original price. What was the machine's original price?

(A) \$326.25
(B) \$348.75
(C) \$409
(D) \$500
(E) \$591

---

20. Ⓐ Ⓑ Ⓒ Ⓓ Ⓔ

225

21. Ⓐ Ⓑ Ⓒ Ⓓ Ⓔ

 DO YOUR FIGURING HERE

BC　　$A = Bx + BC - Dx$

$\dfrac{A - BC}{B - D} = Bx - Dx$

Answer #20: Ⓐ

Concept: • Solving literal equations

An equation which contains letters instead of numbers is called a literal equation. Literal equations are solved by using the same rules as regular equations; just consider each letter as a constant and proceed to solve for x. Thus,

$$A = B(x + C) - Dx$$

$$A = Bx + BC - Dx \qquad \text{Distribute } B$$

$$Bx - Dx = A - BC \qquad \text{Collect common terms}$$

$$x(B - D) = A - BC \qquad \text{Factor the left hand side}$$

$$x = \frac{(A - BC)}{(B - D)} \qquad \text{Divide by B} - \text{D}$$

Answer #21: Ⓓ

Concept: • Solving percent problems

Formula: • $\text{Whole} = \dfrac{\text{part}}{\text{percent}}$

Recall that every percent problem involves three quantities, a *whole* (in this case the original, whole price of the fax machine), a *part* (the part of the original price that the machine was sold for, that is, $225), and a percent (in this problem, 45%). Thus, in this problem, we know the part and the percent and we are looking for the whole. The whole is equal to the part divided by the percent. Thus,

$$\text{Original price} = \frac{225}{45\%} = \frac{225}{0.45} = \$500.$$

This is a good time to remind you that frequently answers to ACT questions can be determined by making a good estimate. In this problem, $225 is 45% of the original price. If, for example, the percent had been 50% instead of 45%, the answer would have been $450. Since we were, in fact, given 45% to work with, the original price must be slightly higher than $450. $500 seems to be the only reasonable answer.

22.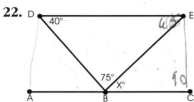

Find the value of x if DE $||$ AC.

(A) 40°
(B) 52.5°
(C) 60°
(D) 65°
(E) 70°

22. (A)   (B)   (C)   (D)   (E)

 DO YOUR FIGURING HERE

Answer #22: Ⓓ

Concept: • Parallel lines
Formula: • Any two alternate interior angles are equal
Definition: • Transversal, alternate interior angles

There are two fundamental geometric facts that are used in solving this problem. First of all, recall that a straight angle (straight line) contains 180°. Secondly, remember that whenever two parallel lines are cut by a transversal, the alternate interior angles are congruent.

Using the fact about alternate interior angles, we can see that angle *DBA* = 40°. And, since *AC* is a straight line, 40° + 75° + $x°$ = 180°. It is easy to see that $x = 65°$.

23. The H. Krauser Company spends 12% of its $42,000 advertising budget on radio advertisements. How much does the company spend on radio advertisements?

    (A) $3,500
    (B) $4,175
    (C) $5,040
    (D) $6,825
    (E) $7,000

23.

 **DO YOUR FIGURING HERE**

Answer #23: Ⓒ

Concept: • Solving percent problems
Formula: • Part = percent × whole

In this percent problem, we have the *whole* (the total advertising budget, $42,000), and the *percent* (12%). We are looking for the *part* of the ad budget that is spent on radio ads. A *part* is always found by multiplying the *percent* times the *whole*. Thus,

$42,000 × 12% = $42,000 × .12 = $5,040.

24. In the right triangle *PQR* below, what is the value of cos *Q*?

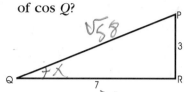

(A) ⅔

(B) ¾

(C) $\dfrac{\sqrt{58}}{7}$

(D) $\dfrac{7\sqrt{58}}{58}$

(E) $\dfrac{3\sqrt{58}}{58}$

SOH
CAH
TOA

$3^2 + 7^2 = c^2$

$9 + 49$

$7^2 + 3^2 =$

$49 + 9$

$7\sqrt{58}$

$\sqrt{58}\sqrt{5}$

$\cos Q = \dfrac{7}{}$

---

24.   Ⓐ   Ⓑ   Ⓒ   ⬤   Ⓔ

  DO YOUR FIGURING HERE

Answer #24: Ⓓ

Concept: • Solving right triangles

Formula: • $\text{Cos } Q = \dfrac{\text{adjacent}}{\text{hypotenuse}}$

In a right triangle, the cosine of an angle is equal to the ratio of the adjacent side to the hypotenuse. In the given triangle, we can use the Pythagorean Theorem to find the value of the hypotenuse.

$$3^2 + 7^2 = b^2$$

$$9 + 49 = b^2$$

$$58 = b^2 \qquad \text{Therefore,}$$

$$b = \sqrt{58} \qquad \text{Then,}$$

$$\cos Q = \frac{\text{adjacent}}{\text{hypotenuse}} = \frac{7}{\sqrt{58}} = \frac{7\sqrt{58}}{58}.$$

25. A department store that employs 275 people hires an additional 20% for the holiday season. What is the total number of employees needed for the holiday season?

(A) 55
(B) 325
(C) 330
(D) 335
(E) 340

26. Nora is now four times as old as Charlie. In one year, Nora will be three times as old as Charlie will be then. How old was Nora three years ago?

(A) 5
(B) 6
(C) 7
(D) 8
(E) 9

---

25. (A) (B) (C) (D) (E)

26. (A) (B) (C) (D) (E)

 DO YOUR FIGURING HERE

275

$N = 4x$

$N = Nora$
$C = charlie$

4

$4c = N$
$N = 3c$

Answer #25: Ⓒ

Concept: • Finding the new value after a percent of increase

Formula: • New value = original value × (100% + percent of increase)

Again, there are two ways to proceed with this problem. Perhaps the more obvious way is to determine the number of additional employees hired, and add this to 275:

Number of new employees = 275 × 20% = 55

Total number of employees = 55 + 275 = 330

The problem can also be solved in just one step by realizing that the total number of employees is 120% (that is, 100% plus 20% more) of the initial number of employees. Thus,

Total number of employees = 275 × 120% = 330.

Answer #26: Ⓐ

Concept: • Solving age problems

There are two unknowns in this problem, Nora's age and Charlie's age. To solve age problems, simply keep track of how old everyone is at each point in time in the problem.

Let N = Nora's age now

Let C = Charlie's age now

Then,

$N + 1$ = Nora's age in 1 year

$C + 1$ = Charlie's age in 1 year

Right now, Nora is four times as old as Charlie. This means that $N = 4C$ We also know that in 1 year Nora will be 3 times as old as Charlie. Thus, in 1 year,

$N + 1 = 3 (C + 1)$ Distribute the 3

$N + 1 = 3C + 3$ or,

$N = 3C + 2$ Now, substitute $N = 4C$ into this equation

$4C = 3C + 2$

$C = 2$

Thus, right now, Charlie is 2. This tells us that right now, Nora is 8. And three years ago, she was 5.

27. A mattress and boxspring set, which originally sells for $460, is marked down 20%, and then the discounted price is marked down an additional 10%. What is the final sale price?

(A) $331.20
(B) $322
(C) $358.80
(D) $404.80
(E) $414.00

28. Three business partners share the profits of their company in a ratio of 6:5:4. This year, the total profits were $1,200,000. Find the amount received by the partner who got the largest share.

(A) $300,000
(B) $320,000
(C) $400,000
(D) $480,000
(E) $520,000

27. (A) (B) (C) (D) (E)

28. (A) (B) (C) (D) (E)

 DO YOUR FIGURING HERE

2222
6 : 5 : 4

400,000 :

4 60

6 : 5:4

Answer #27: Ⓐ

Concept: • Successive discounts
Formula: • Final price = original price × (100% − first percent of discount) × (100% − second percent of discount)

Again, it makes sense to begin by showing the common error that many people make. Frequently, the thinking is that a discount of 20% followed by a discount of 10% is equivalent to a discount of 30%. Thus, the final price would be 70% of the original.

$460 − (30%) $460 = (70%) × $460 = $322.

The reason that this is incorrect is that the second discount is taken after the first discount, and is thus a markdown from an already reduced amount. The problem must be done in two steps. First, find the price after the 20% discount (which is 80% of the original price).

$460 × 80% = $368.

Now, this price must be reduced by 10%.

$365 × 90% = $331.20

Answer #28: Ⓓ

Definition: • Ratios

While it is possible to solve this problem algebraically, it is a lot easier to proceed arithmetically. To proceed arithmetically, one must simply understand that one way to picture a ratio of 6:5:4 is to consider the money divided up into 15 equal pieces (15 = 6 + 5 + 4). The largest share is equivalent to 6 of these 15 parts, that is, $\frac{6}{15}$ of the total amount. Then,

$1,200,000 × ($\frac{6}{15}$) = $480,000.

29. A circle has a radius of R and an area of X. In terms of X, what is the area of a circle with radius $3R$?

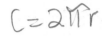

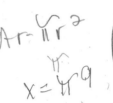

(A) $3X^2$
(B) $9X^2$
(C) $9X$
(D) $3X$
(E) 9

29. (A) (B) (C) (D) (E)

 DO YOUR FIGURING HERE

Answer #29: ⓒ

Concept: • Radius, area of a circle
Formula: • $A = \pi r^2$

Recall that the formula for the area of a circle is $A = \pi r^2$. In this problem, the radius is R and the area is X. Thus, for our circle, $X = \pi R^2$.

Now, if the radius of the circle had been $3R$ instead, the area would be $\pi(3R)^2$, or $9\pi R^2$.

You can see from this that if the radius of a circle is tripled, the area is multiplied by 9. Since the area of the circle with radius R is X, the area of the circle with radius $3R$ is $9X$.

30. Perform the indicated operation and express the result in lowest terms:

$$\frac{x^2 - 36}{x^2} \div \frac{3x + 18}{x}$$

(A) $\frac{(x - 6)}{3x}$

(B) $\frac{(x + 6)}{3x}$

(C) $\frac{(x - 6)}{3}$

(D) $\frac{3}{(x - 6)}$

(E) $\frac{(x + 6)}{3}$

Handwritten work:
$$\frac{\cancel{x+6} \;\; x-6}{\cancel{x^2}} \cdot \frac{\cancel{x}}{3\cancel{(x+6)}}$$

$$\frac{x^2 - 6x}{x - 6}$$
$$\frac{x - 6}{x}$$

30. Ⓐ Ⓑ Ⓒ Ⓓ Ⓔ

 DO YOUR FIGURING HERE

Answer #30: Ⓐ

Concept: • Algebraic fractions

To divide fractions, you must "invert and multiply."

$$\frac{x^2 - 36}{x^2} \cdot \frac{x}{3x + 18}$$

Now, factor all terms:

$$\frac{(x - 6)(x + 6)}{x^2} \cdot \frac{x}{3(x + 6)}$$

Cancel common factors

$$\frac{(x - 6)\cancel{(x + 6)}}{x^{\cancel{2}}} \cdot \frac{\cancel{x}}{3\cancel{(x + 6)}} = \frac{x - 6}{3x}$$

31. Express 0.005 as a percent

    (A) 0.00005%
    (B) 0.0005%
    (C) 0.005%
    (D) 0.05%
    (E) 0.5%

32. $6^3 - 4^2 =$

    (A) 2
    (B) 10
    (C) 32
    (D) 200
    (E) 208

31. Ⓐ Ⓑ Ⓒ Ⓓ Ⓔ

32. Ⓐ Ⓑ Ⓒ ● Ⓔ

 DO YOUR FIGURING HERE

Answer #31: Ⓔ

Concept: • Writing decimals as percents
Definition: • Percents

Recall that "percent" means "per hundred." To change any decimal to a percent, you simply need to multiply or, equivalently, move the decimal two places to the right. Thus,

$$0.005 \times 100 = 0.5\%$$

Answer #32: Ⓓ

Concept: • Evaluating numbers with exponents

In this problem, you must avoid the common tendency to make up rules that do not exist. There is really no useful way to simplify the given expression by combining the two terms 6^3 and 4^2. Instead, evaluate 6^3 and 4^2, and then subtract. Thus,

$$6^3 - 4^2 = 216 - 16 = 200$$

33. If $\dfrac{x}{7} - \dfrac{x}{5} > 3$, then a possible value of x is

(A) −53
(B) −52
(C) −51
(D) 52
(E) 53

7.428

−7.285714286

34. If the radius of a circle is tripled, then

(A) The circumference and the area are both tripled
(B) The circumference is tripled and the area is multiplied by 6
(C) The circumference is tripled and the area is multiplied by 9
(D) The circumference is multiplied by 9 and the area is multiplied by 6
(E) The circumference and the area are both multiplied by 9

33. Ⓐ Ⓑ Ⓒ Ⓓ Ⓔ

34. Ⓐ Ⓑ Ⓒ Ⓓ Ⓔ

DO YOUR FIGURING HERE

$C = 6\pi$ $A = 9\pi$

$C = 2\pi(27)$ $\pi\,27^2$

$= 54\pi$ $= 729$

$C = 2\pi\,3r$

$C = 2\pi\,27$

54

$A = \pi r^2$

$C = 2\pi\,3$

$C = 6\pi$ $A = \pi 9$

$A = \pi(3)^2$

Answer #33: Ⓐ

Concept: • Solving inequalities

To find which of the above numbers is a possible value of x, we need to solve the inequality. Remember that solving inequalities is exactly the same as solving equations with one exception: whenever you multiply or divide by a negative number, you must change the direction of the inequality. Thus,

$$\frac{x}{7} - \frac{x}{5} > 3 \qquad \text{Multiply by 35 (The LCD of 5 and 7)}$$

$5x - 7x > 105$ Or,

$-2x > 105$ Divide by -2, and flip the inequality sign.

$x < -52.5$

The only number given that is less than -52.5 is -53.

Answer #34: Ⓒ

Concept: • Circumference, area
Formula: • $C = 2\pi r$, $A = \pi r^2$

To start, you must know the formulas for the circumference and the area of a circle. The formula for the circumference is $C = 2\pi r$, and the formula for the area is $A = \pi r^2$, where, of course, r represents the radius of the circle.

Now, if you triple the radius, the circumference becomes $C = 2\pi(3r) = 6\pi r$, which is three times as big as $2\pi r$. Thus, if you triple the radius, the circumference is also tripled.

However, when you triple the radius, the area becomes $A = \pi(3r)^2 = 9\pi r^2$, which is 9 times as big as πr^2. Thus, if you triple the radius, the area is multiplied by 9.

35. A coin purse contains 7 pennies, 4 nickels, and 5 dimes. If one coin is removed from the purse at random, what is the probability that the coin is either a dime or a penny?

(A) ⅜
(B) ⅝
(C) ⅔
(D) ¾
(E) ⅘

36. Simplify $(3a^3b^2c)^4$

(A) $12a^7b^8c^5$
(B) $27a^{12}b^8c^4$
(C) $81a^{12}b^8c^4$
(D) $12a^{12}b^8c^4$
(E) $81a^7b^8c^5$

---

35. Ⓐ Ⓑ Ⓒ Ⓓ Ⓔ $81a^{12}b^8c4$

36. Ⓐ Ⓑ Ⓒ Ⓓ Ⓔ

 DO YOUR FIGURING HERE

$12/16$

7 pennies $3/4$
4 nickels   16
5 dimes

Answer #35: Ⓓ

Concept: • Basic probability
Formula: • The probability of a success =

$$\frac{\text{(The number of successful outcomes)}}{\text{(The total number of outcomes)}}$$

The act of picking a dime or a penny from the purse is called a "success," and we wish to determine the probability of a success. The formula is simply

The probability of a success =

$$\frac{\text{(The number of successful outcomes)}}{\text{(The total number of outcomes)}}$$

The total number of different outcomes when selecting from the purse is $7 + 4 + 5 = 16$. The total number of successes is $7 + 5 = 12$. Thus,

The probability of a success = $^{12}\!/_{16} = \,^{3}\!/_{4}$.

Answer #36: Ⓒ

Concept: • Evaluating expressions with exponents
Formula: • $(xy)^n = x^n y^n$ and $(x^n)^m = x^{nm}$

Two of the fundamental properties for working with exponents are needed to simplify the given expression. Recall:

$(xy)^n = x^n y^n$ and

$(x^n)^m = x^{nm}$ Thus,

$(3a^3b^2c)^4 = 3^4(a^3)^4(b^2)^4(c^1)^4 = 81a^{12}b^8c^4$

37. Solve for x:

$9 + 4 =$

$$\left(\frac{3}{4}\right)x + \left(\frac{x}{3}\right) = 13$$

(A) 12
(B) 13
(C) 24
(D) 30⅓
(E) 39

$\frac{3}{4}x + \frac{x}{3} = 13$

$18 + 6 =$

9.75

38. If $a = 2$, $b = -3$, and $c = -4$, what is the value of

$$\frac{\sqrt{b^2 + ac}}{c - b}\,?$$

(A) $-\sqrt{17}$ $\sqrt{(-3)^2 + 2(-4)}$

(B) -1

(C) 1

(D) $\dfrac{\sqrt{17}}{7}$ $\sqrt{9 + -8}$

(E) $\sqrt{17}$ $\sqrt{\dfrac{1}{-4 - -3}}$

$\left(\dfrac{\sqrt{1}}{-1}\right)^2$

$\dfrac{+}{1}$

37. Ⓐ Ⓑ Ⓒ Ⓓ Ⓔ

38. Ⓐ Ⓑ Ⓒ Ⓓ Ⓔ

 DO YOUR FIGURING HERE

Answer #37: Ⓐ

Concept: • Solving equations with fractions

It is extremely common for people to make mistakes when dealing with fractions, and so, it is advisable when attempting to solve an equation with fractions, to get rid of the fractions immediately. This can be accomplished by multiplying both sides of the equation by the LCD of the fractions. In this problem the LCD is 12. Thus,

$$\left(\frac{3}{4}\right)x + \left(\frac{x}{3}\right) = 13 \quad \text{Multiply by 12}$$

$$12\left(\frac{3}{4}\right)x + 12\left(\frac{x}{3}\right) = (13)(12) \quad \text{or}$$

$$9x + 4x = 156 \qquad\qquad \text{Then,}$$

$$13x = 156 \qquad\qquad \text{and,}$$

$$x = 12$$

Answer #38: Ⓑ

Concept: • Evaluating algebraic expressions

Begin by plugging the given values for a, b, and c into the given expression.

$$\frac{\sqrt{(-3)^2 + (2)(-4)}}{-4 - (-3)}$$

Now, carefully evaluate the expression, paying particular attention to the rules of sign.

$$\frac{\sqrt{9 + (-8)}}{-4 + (+3)} = \frac{\sqrt{1}}{-1} = \frac{1}{-1} = -1$$

39. The solutions of the equation $3x^2 + 13x - 10 = 0$ are

(A) $-\frac{2}{3}$ and $+5$
(B) $-\frac{2}{3}$ and -5
(C) $+\frac{2}{3}$ and $+5$
(D) $+\frac{2}{3}$ and -5
(E) $\frac{3}{2}$ and -5

40. The expression $\sqrt{405}$ is the same as

(A) $9\sqrt{5}$
(B) $81\sqrt{5}$
(C) $5\sqrt{9}$
(D) $5\sqrt{3}$
(E) $3\sqrt{5}$

39. (A) (B) (C) (D) (E)

40. (A) (B) (C) (D) (E)

 DO YOUR FIGURING HERE

$\sqrt{405}$ $\begin{smallmatrix}5 & 81 \\ & \wedge \\ & 9 \ 9\end{smallmatrix}$

$9\sqrt{5}$

$3x^2 + 13x - 10 = 0$

$(3x - 2)(x + 5)$

$x = 2/3$

$-5 \quad 3x - 2 = 0$

Answer #39   Ⓓ

Concept: • Solving quadratic equations
Definition: • Quadratic equations

Whenever you need to solve a quadratic equation on the ACT, begin by rewriting the equation so that all of the terms are combined on the left, and the right side is equal to 0. In this particular problem, this has already been done. Next, determine if the left side can be factored. If it can, the problem can easily be solved by setting each factor equal to 0 and solving the resulting equations. If not, we have to solve the equation by the quadratic formula. In this problem, we are able to factor:

$3x^2 + 13x - 10 = 0$ Factor the left handside

$(3x - 2)(x + 5) = 0$ Set each factor equal to 0 and solve

$3x - 2 = 0 \quad x + 5 = 0$

$3x = 2 \quad\quad x = -5$

$x = \frac{2}{3}$

The two solutions are $\frac{2}{3}$ and -5.

Answer #40:   Ⓐ

Concept: • Simplifying square roots

To simplify a square root in the easiest possible way, begin by prime factoring the number under the radical sign.

$405 = 81 \times 5 = 9 \times 9 \times 5 = 3 \times 3 \times 3 \times 3 \times 5$ Thus,

$$\sqrt{405} = \sqrt{3 \times 3 \times 3 \times 3 \times 5}$$

Now, simply look for any repeated factors under the radical sign. Any factors that appear twice under the radical sign should be removed from under the sign and positioned *once* outside of the sign. For example, in this problem, each pair of 3s under the radical becomes one 3 on the outside. Thus,

$$\sqrt{405} = \sqrt{3 \times 3 \times 3 \times 3 \times 5} = (3)(3)\sqrt{5} = 9\sqrt{5}$$

41. The line graph below is the graph of which of the following inequalities?

(A) $-4 \le x < 3$ $-4 < x \le 3$
(B) $-4 < x < 3$
(C) $-4 \le x \le 3$
(D) $-4 < x \le 3$
(E) $x < -4$ or $x \ge 3$

41. (A) (B) (C) (D) (E)

 DO YOUR FIGURING HERE

Answer #41: Ⓓ

Definition: • Open set, closed set, interval notation

Clearly, the line graph is indicating the set of points between −4 and +3. The only tricky part is remembering the meaning of the open and closed dots on either end of the graph.

An open dot indicates that the endpoint *is not* a value of the indicated set, while a closed dot indicates that the indicated point *is* a value of the indicated set. Thus, on this graph, the endpoint −4 is not included, while the endpoint 3 is included. In other words, the indicated set is all points between −4 and +3, including +3, but not −4. This is indicated as $-4 < x \le 3$.

42. Find the common solution of
the two equations:

$$2x + 5y = 2$$
$$3x - 5y = 13$$

(A) $(3, -\frac{4}{5})$
(B) $(-3, \frac{5}{4})$
(C) $(3, \frac{4}{5})$
(D) $(-3, \frac{4}{5})$
(E) None of these

$$+\ \ 2x + 5y = 2$$
$$3x - 5y = 13$$
$$\overline{}$$
$$5x = 15$$
$$x = 3$$

42. Ⓐ Ⓑ Ⓒ Ⓓ Ⓔ

✍ **DO YOUR FIGURING HERE**

$$2(3) + 5y = 2$$

$$6 + 5y = 2$$
$$-6$$

$$5y = \frac{-4}{5}$$

$$3, -\frac{4}{5}$$

Answer #42: Ⓐ

Concept: • Solving a system of equations
Definition: • Addition method, substitution method

There are two techniques that can be used to find the common solution of a set of two equations in two unknowns, the substitution method (solve one of the equations for one unknown, and plug the value obtained into the other equation), and the addition method (add the two equations together in such a way as to eliminate one of the unknowns). The two equations that are given here are custom-made for the addition method, since, when they are added together, the variable y "adds out." Thus,

$$2x + 5y = 2$$
$$3x - 5y = 13 \quad \text{Add the equations together}$$
$$5x = 15 \quad \text{Solve for } x$$
$$x = 3$$

Plug $x = 3$ into the first equation to find the value of y

$$2x + 5y = 2$$
$$2(3) + 5y = 2 \quad \text{Solve for } y$$
$$6 + 5y = 2$$
$$5y = -4$$
$$y = -\tfrac{4}{5}$$

The common solution is $(3, -\tfrac{4}{5})$

43. In right triangle DEF, with angle F a right angle, csc D = $^{13}/_{12}$. What is the value of tan D?

(A) $^{5}/_{13}$
(B) $^{5}/_{12}$
(C) $^{12}/_{13}$
(D) $^{12}/_{5}$
(E) $^{13}/_{5}$

44. If a function f is defined as $f(x) = x^3 - 4x^2 - 21x$, find all of the values of x such that $f(x) = 0$.

(A) 7, −3
(B) 0, 7, −3
(C) 0, −7, 3
(D) 3, −7
(E) 0, −3, 3

SOH CAH TOA

43. (A) (B) (C) (D) (E)

44. (A) (B) (C) (D) (E)

 **DO YOUR FIGURING HERE**

CSC

H/O

12/5

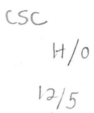

$12^2 + x^2 = 13^2$

$144 + x^2 = 169$

$7^3 - 4(7)^2 - 21(7)$
$343 - 196 - 147$

$-3^3 - 4(-3)^2 - 21($
$-27 - -36 - -63$

$-27 - 36 - -63$

-63

O

Answer #43: Ⓓ

Concept: • Evaluating trigonometric functions in a right triangle

Formula: • Tan D = $\dfrac{\text{opposite}}{\text{adjacent}}$

In a right triangle, the csc of an angle is equal to the hypotenuse divided by the side opposite the angle. Since we know csc D = $^{13}\!/_{12}$, we know that the triangle in question has a hypotenuse of 13, and the side opposite angle D is 12.

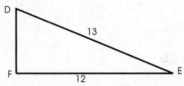

The Pythagorean theorem can be used to determine that the missing (adjacent) side is 5. Now, the tangent of an angle is the ratio of the opposite side to the adjacent side. Thus,

$$\tan D = \frac{\text{opposite}}{\text{adjacent}} = \frac{12}{5}$$

Answer #44: Ⓑ

Concept: • Functional notation
Definition: • Functions

$f(x) = 0$ when $x^3 - 4x^2 - 21x = 0$. The equation we must solve here is a cubic equation. While, in general, there is no "nice" way to solve cubic equations, this one can readily be solved by noticing that a common factor of x can be removed from each term.

$x^3 - 4x^2 - 21x = 0$ Factor x from each term on the left hand side

$x(x^2 - 4x - 21) = 0$

Now, we must solve the quadratic in parentheses. Luckily, it factors easily.

$x(x - 7)(x + 3) = 0$

Set each factor equal to 0, and solve the resulting equations

$$x = 0 \qquad x - 7 = 0 \qquad x + 3 = 0$$
$$x = 7 \qquad\quad x = -3$$

Thus, $f(x) = 0$ when $x = 0$, 7, or -3.

45. A circle is inscribed in a
square whose side is 12.
What is the circumference of
the circle (in terms of π)?

(A) 3π
(B) 6π
(C) 12π
(D) 18π
(E) 36π

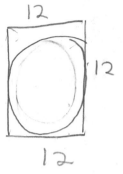

12

12

12

12

12

45. (A) (B) (C) (D) (E)

$2\pi r$

$C = 2\pi r$

$12 = 2\pi r$
$\overline{2}$

✎ **DO YOUR FIGURING HERE**

Answer #45: Ⓒ

Concept: • Circumference
Formula: • C = 2πr
Definition: • Inscribed

Frequently, when trying to solve a geometry problem that does not contain a diagram, it is a very good idea to sketch the diagram yourself. In this problem the diagram, shown below, gives the problem away.

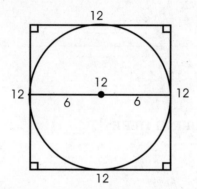

Clearly the circle in the drawing has a diameter that is the same as the side of the square, that is, 12. The radius of the circle, then, is 6. And, since the formula for the circumference of a circle is C = 2πr, the circumference is 12π.

46. If the average (arithmetic mean) of 15, 8, and Q is 9, what is the value of Q?

(A) 3
(B) 4
(C) 5
(D) 6
(E) 7

46.   (A)   (B)   (C)   (D)   (E)

 **DO YOUR FIGURING HERE**

$$(3) \ \frac{15+8+X}{3} = 9 \ (3)$$

$$15+8+X = 27$$

$$X = 4$$

Answer #46: Ⓑ

Concept: • Finding averages

Formula: • Average = $\dfrac{\text{sum of all quantities}}{\text{number of quantities}}$

There are two methods that can be used to solve this problem, an algebraic method and a counting method. First of all, let's solve the problem algebraically. By the definition of average, we have

$$\frac{15 + 8 + Q}{3} = 9 \quad \text{Multiply by 3}$$

$$15 + 8 + Q = 27 \quad \text{or,}$$

$$23 + Q = 27 \quad \text{so}$$

$$Q = 4$$

The counting method is generally quicker. Simply keep track of how much above and below the average each given number is, and you will know what the value of the missing number must be. In this case, 15 is 6 above the average of 9, and 8 is 1 below the average of 9. Together, the two numbers are, then, 5 above the average. Then, it must be the case that the remaining number is 5 below the average. And, the number that is 5 below 9 is 4.

The next two questions are based on the graph below:

The Wilson Family Budget

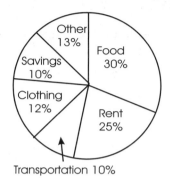

47. What fractional part of its monthly budget does the Wilson family spend on clothing?

    (A) ³⁄₂₅
    (B) ⅛
    (C) ¹³⁄₁₀₀
    (D) ⁹⁄₂₅
    (E) ⁴⁄₉

    12/100

    3/25

48. If the Wilsons' monthly income is $2,600, how much is budgeted for rent?

    (A) $260
    (B) $520
    (C) $620
    (D) $650
    (E) $975

---

47. Ⓐ Ⓑ Ⓒ Ⓓ Ⓔ

48. Ⓐ Ⓑ Ⓒ Ⓓ Ⓔ

 **DO YOUR FIGURING HERE**

Answer #47: Ⓐ

Concept: • Writing percents as fractions

Formula: • $A\% = \dfrac{A}{100}$

This is a very straightforward question. The Wilson family spends 12% of its monthly budget on clothing, so we simply need to express 12% as a fraction, and reduce it.

$$12\% = \frac{12}{100} = \frac{6}{50} = \frac{3}{25}$$

Answer #48: Ⓓ

Concept: • Solving percent problems

Formula: • Part = whole × percent

This is essentially a percent problem in which the whole is 2,600 and the percent is 25%. To find the part of their monthly income spent on rent, simply multiply.

$$2{,}600 \times 25\% = 2{,}600 \times 0.25 = 650$$

49. What is the perimeter of the square whose diagonal is $8\sqrt{2}$?

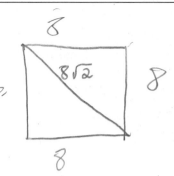

(A) 8
(B) 16
(C) 32
(D) $32\sqrt{2}$
(E) 64

49. (A) (B) (C) (D) (E)

 DO YOUR FIGURING HERE

$$a^2 + b^2 = \left(8\sqrt{2}\right)^2$$

$$8\sqrt{2} \times 8\sqrt{2}$$

$$64 \cdot 2$$

$$128$$

Answer #49: Ⓒ

Concept: • Pythagorean Theorem
Formula: • $a^2 + b^2 = c^2$
Definition: • Perimeter

Begin by making a sketch of the square. Call the sides of the square x.

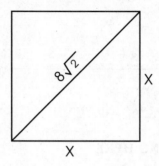

Then, we can use the Pythagorean Theorem to determine the value of x.

$$x^2 + x^2 = (8\sqrt{2})^2$$

$$2x^2 = 128$$

$$x^2 = 64$$

$$x = 8$$

Knowing that the side of the square is 8, it can easily be seen that the perimeter is $4(8) = 32$.

50. Each of the 60 students in the first grade contributed either a nickel or a quarter to the school food drive. If the total amount contributed was $9.40, how many students contributed a nickel?

(A) 26
(B) 28
(C) 30
(D) 32
(E) 34

50. Ⓐ Ⓑ Ⓒ Ⓓ Ⓔ

 DO YOUR FIGURING HERE

$.5x + .25y = 9.40$

$5x + 25y = 940$

$- \ 5x + 5y = -300$

$20y = 640$

$y = 32$

Answer #50: Ⓑ

Concept: • Solving algebraic word problems with two unknowns
Formula: • (Amount of contribution) × (number of contributors) = total contributed

There are two unknowns in this problem, the number of students who contributed a nickel and the number of students who contributed a quarter. We also are given enough information to write two equations. Once we have written the two equations, we can solve them to find their common solution.

Let N = the number of students who contributed a nickel
Let Q = the number of students who contributed a quarter

Then, $N + Q = 60$

and, $.05N + .25Q = 9.40$

Let's solve these equations by using the substitution method. The first equation can be rewritten as $N = 60 - Q$. Plug this into the second equation and solve.

$.05N + .25Q = 9.40$ Substitute $N = 60 - Q$

$.05(60 - Q) + .25Q = 9.40$ Distribute

$3 - .05Q + .25Q = 9.40$ Then,

$.2Q = 6.40$ And, dividing by .2,

$Q = 32.$

Then, $N = 60 - Q = 60 - 32 = 28$

Thus, 28 students contributed a nickel.

51. A shoe store advertises a pair of shoes for $60. This price was 120% of the price at a competing shoe store. What was the price at the competitor's store?

(A) $48
(B) $50
(C) $70
(D) $72
(E) $75

52. Mr. Tower takes 8 hours to drive from New York City to Buffalo. What fractional part of the drive still remains after he has driven x hours?

(A) $\dfrac{x}{8}$

(B) $\dfrac{8}{x}$

(C) $\dfrac{8 - x}{x}$

(D) $\dfrac{8 - x}{8}$

(E) $\dfrac{x - 8}{x}$

51. (A) (B) (C) (D) (E)

52. (A) (B) (C) (D) (E)

 DO YOUR FIGURING HERE

68

Answer #51: Ⓑ

Concept: • Finding the original value before a percent of increase

Formula: • Original value = $\dfrac{\text{new value}}{(100\% + \text{percent of increase})}$

Let's begin by looking at a very common mistake that people make when trying to solve problems such as this one.

Figuring that the price of the shoes ($60) is 120% of the competing price, people often simply take the $60 and reduce it by 20%. This would yield

$$\$60 - (20\%)\,\$60 = (80\%)\,\$60 = \$48.$$

Thus, many people choose solution A. The reason this is incorrect is that the percentage given in the problem is a percentage of the competing price, and NOT a percentage of the $60. Thus, it is incorrect to apply the percent to the $60.

Instead, think algebraically. Let C = the competitor's price. Then, 120% of this price is $60.

$$120\% \times C = 60 \quad \text{Divide by 120\%}$$

$$C = \frac{60}{120\%} = \frac{60}{1.2} = 50.$$

Answer #52: Ⓓ

Concept: • Computing with algebraic fractions

Formula: • Fraction remaining = 1 − fraction used

After x hours, Mr. Tower will have driven $\dfrac{x}{8}$ of the drive. The part of the drive that still remains, therefore, is

$$1 - \left(\frac{x}{8}\right) = \left(\frac{8}{8}\right) - \left(\frac{x}{8}\right) = \frac{(8 - x)}{8}$$

53. What is the area of the parallelogram shown below?

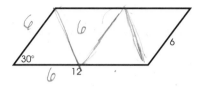

(A) 18

(B) $18\sqrt{2}$

(C) $18\sqrt{3}$

(D) 36

(E) $36\sqrt{2}$

53. (A) (B) (C) (D) (E)

✏️ **DO YOUR FIGURING HERE**

Answer #53: Ⓓ

Concept: • 30-60-90 triangles, area of a parallelogram
Formula: • A = bh

The area of a parallelogram is equal to the base times the height. The height is the length of the line segment labeled *h* in the figure below.

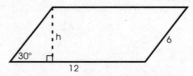

The value of *h* can be determined by noting that the triangle in the figure above is a 30-60-90 triangle with hypotenuse 6. In such a triangle, the length of the side opposite the 30° angle (which is *h*) is one half of the hypotenuse. Thus, *h* = 3, and the area is

A = bh = 12 × 3 = 36

54. Of the 200 members of a club, 30% are women, and of these, ¼ are new members. If the number of men that are new members is three times the number of women that are new members, how many men are new members?

60

15 X 3

200

(A) 15
(B) 30
(C) 45
(D) 60
(E) 75

54. Ⓐ Ⓑ ⬤ Ⓓ Ⓔ

 DO YOUR FIGURING HERE

Answer #54: Ⓒ

Concept: • Computing with fractions and percents

Formula: • Part = percent × whole or part = fraction × whole

This problem is really just a "bookkeeping" problem. Keep track of all of the numbers in the problem, and the solution will fall right out. First of all, let's find out how many women are in the club.

200 × 30% = 60

Thus, there are 60 women in the club. Now, ¼ of this number is 15, so there were 15 new female members. Three times this number will give us the number of men that are new members. Thus, there are 45 men that are new members.

55. If $2x + 5y = 12$, then
$6x + 15y =$

(A) 18
(B) 24
(C) 30
(D) 36
(E) It cannot be deter-
mined.

56. The value of an investment after one year was $24,000. The increase in value during the year was $6,000. What was the percent of increase in the value of the investment?

(A) 25%
(B) 33⅓%
(C) 40%
(D) 66⅔%
(E) 75%

55. Ⓐ Ⓑ Ⓒ Ⓓ Ⓔ

56. Ⓐ Ⓑ Ⓒ Ⓓ Ⓔ

 DO YOUR FIGURING HERE

$2x + 5y = 12$

Answer #55: Ⓓ

Concept: • Manipulating algebraic expressions (properties of equations)

This is a very tricky question, yet one that is very easy to answer once you know the trick. Most people answer (E), since they know that you cannot solve a single equation with two unknowns. However, note that the expression you are asked to evaluate, $6x + 15y$, is a multiple of the expression whose value you are given. That is, $2x + 5y = 12$, and thus $3(2x + 5y) = 3(12)$. This means that $6x + 15y = 3(12) = 36$.

Answer #56: Ⓑ

Concept: • Finding a percent of increase

Formula: • Percent of increase $= \dfrac{\text{amount of change}}{\text{original value}}$

Percent of increase can be easily computed as the amount of change divided by the original value. In this problem, we know the amount of increase is \$6,000. However, we are not given the original value; we have the final value instead. To get the original value, of course, we simply need to subtract: \$24,000 − \$6,000 = \$18,000. Then,

$$\text{Percent of increase} = \frac{\text{change}}{\text{original}} = \frac{6,000}{18,000} = \frac{6}{18} = \frac{1}{3} = 33\frac{1}{3}\%.$$

57. If the angles of a given triangle are in the ratio of 2 : 3 : 4, the triangle is

   (A) Isosceles
   (B) Equilateral
   (C) Right
   (D) Acute
   (E) Obtuse

58. An investment of $7,000 earns $800 each year. At the same rate, how much must be invested to earn $1,200 a year?

   (A) $3,500
   (B) $9,600
   (C) $9,800
   (D) $10,500
   (E) $10,800

57. (A) (B) (C) (D) (E)

$7,000$
$+$

58. (A) (B) (C) ● (E)

 DO YOUR FIGURING HERE

Answer #57: Ⓓ

Concept: • Ratios, 180° in a triangle
Definition: • Isosceles, equilateral, acute, obtuse, right triangle

One of the easiest ways to view a ratio of 2 : 3 : 4 is to consider the 180° of the triangle as divided up into $2 + 3 + 4 = 9$ parts. Then, one of the angles of the triangle is $\frac{2}{9}$ of the 180°, one is $\frac{3}{9}$ of the 180°, and one is $\frac{4}{9}$ of the 180°. Thus, the three angles of the triangle are

$$\left(\frac{2}{9}\right) \times 180 = 40°$$

$$\left(\frac{3}{9}\right) \times 180 = 60°$$

$$\left(\frac{4}{9}\right) \times 180 = 80°$$

An acute triangle is one in which all three angles are less than 90°

Answer #58: Ⓓ

Concept: • Solving proportions
Formula: • $\dfrac{a}{b} = \dfrac{c}{d}$ implies $a \times d = b \times c$
Definition: • Proportions

This is a straightforward direct proportion problem, in which we need to determine "800 is to 7,000 as 1,200 is to ?" Set up a proportion.

$$\frac{800}{7,000} = \frac{1,200}{x}$$

Things become a bit easier at this point if you cancel two zeros from the top and bottom of the first fraction, obtaining

$$\frac{8}{70} = \frac{1,200}{x}$$

Next, cross multiply

$8x = 70 \times 1,200$ Or

$8x = 84,000$ Divide by 8

$x = 10,500$

59. The volume of a rectangular carton with a square base is 36 cubic feet. If the height of the carton is 24 inches, how many feet are there in each side of the base?

(A) $2\sqrt{3}$
(B) $3\sqrt{2}$
(C) 6
(D) 9
(E) 18

60. A vertical antenna tower is supported by a wire that runs from the top of the tower to the ground. If the wire makes an angle of 62° with the ground and is 575 yards long, how tall is the tower?

(A) 575 cos 62°
(B) 575 sin 62°
(C) $\dfrac{575}{\sin 62°}$
(D) $\dfrac{575}{\cos 62°}$
(E) 575 tan 62°

59. (A) (B) (C) (D) (E)

60. (A) (B) (C) (D) (E)

 DO YOUR FIGURING HERE

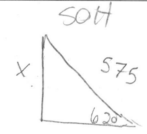

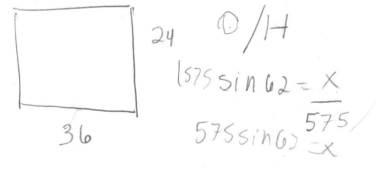

Answer #59: Ⓑ

Concept: • Volume of a rectangular solid
Formula: • V = LWH

One thing to be very careful of in doing this problem is to not mix up the units. Note that while the volume is given in cubic feet, the height is in inches. It is probably safest to convert all quantities to the same units right off the bat, to avoid a mistake later on. Thus, let us express the height of the carton as 2 feet, instead of 24 inches.

Now, the volume of a rectangular solid is given by V = LWH. Since V = 36 and H = 2, we have

   36 = LW(2) or LW = 18

This tells us that the area of the base is 18. Since the base is square, each side would be equal to $\sqrt{18}$.

$$\sqrt{18} = \sqrt{2 \times 9} = 3\sqrt{2}$$

Answer #60: Ⓑ

Concept: • Solving trigonometric word problems

Formula: • $\text{Sin } x° = \dfrac{\text{opposite}}{\text{hypotenuse}}$

The best way to begin this problem is by making a picture of the tower. Let h = the height of the tower.

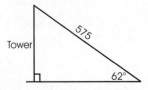

Now, we are looking for h, the side opposite the 62° angle, and we know that the hypotenuse of the triangle is 575. The trigonometric ratio that involves opposite and hypotenuse is sine.

$$\text{Sin } 62° = \frac{\text{opposite}}{\text{hypotenuse}} = \frac{h}{575}$$

   Thus, h = 575 sin 62°

TEST
2

This test consists of sixty questions and five possible answer choices for each. For each problem, select the answer choice that represents the best solution and shade the corresponding oval.

Note: Unless otherwise stated, all of the following should be assumed:

1. Illustrative figures are NOT necessarily drawn to scale.

2. Geometric figures lie on a plane.

3. The word *line* indicates a straight line.

4. The word *average* indicates arithmetic mean.

1. If a certain upholstery material sells for $8.16 a yard, how much will it cost to buy 144 inches of material?

    (A) $2.04
    (B) $16.32
    (C) $24.32
    (D) $32.64
    (E) $65.28

2. Which of the following decimals is equivalent to ¼%?

    (A) 0.00025
    (B) 0.0025
    (C) 0.025
    (D) 0.25
    (E) 2.5

1. Ⓐ Ⓑ Ⓒ ⬤ Ⓔ

2. Ⓐ ⬤ Ⓒ Ⓓ Ⓔ

✍ **DO YOUR FIGURING HERE**

25 %

.0025

8.16   36

4

Answer #1:   Ⓓ

Concept: • Converting units of measure
Formula: • 36 inches = 1 yard

First of all, we must determine the number of yards of material we are buying.

$$\frac{144 \text{ inches}}{36 \text{ inches/yard}} = 4 \text{ yards}$$

4 yards of material @ $8.16 a yard = 4 × $8.16 = $32.64

Answer #2:   Ⓑ

Concept: • Changing percents to decimals

Definition: • $A\% = \dfrac{A}{100}$

Since ¼ is equal to 0.25 when written as a decimal, ¼% = 0.25%. To change a percent to a decimal, simply divide by 100, which is the same as moving the decimal point two places to the left.

$$\frac{1}{4}\% = 0.25\% = \frac{0.25}{100} = 0.0025$$

3. A recent product preference survey showed that 368 out of 400 people tested liked a new product. What percent of the people tested did not like the new product?

   (A) 7%
   (B) 8%
   (C) 9%
   (D) 91%
   (E) 92%

4. If $4P + 7 \leq 6P - 3$, then

   (A) $P \geq 10$
   (B) $P \leq 10$
   (C) $P \leq -5$
   (D) $P \leq 5$
   (E) $P \geq 5$

3. Ⓐ ● Ⓒ Ⓓ Ⓔ

4. Ⓐ Ⓑ Ⓒ Ⓓ ●

DO YOUR FIGURING HERE

$$4P + 7 \leq 6P - 3$$

$$\frac{10}{2} \leq \frac{2P}{2}$$

$$5 \leq P$$

Answer #3: Ⓑ

Concept: • Solving percent problems

Formula: • Percent $= \dfrac{\text{Part}}{\text{Whole}}$

Before even beginning this problem, it is important to make a comment. This is a trick question, in the sense that it talks about the number of people that *liked* a new product, and then asks for the percent of people that *did not* like it. Be sure to read every question on your test very carefully to make sure that you are answering the question that is being asked.

Once you realize the above, there are two ways to proceed. One is to find the percent of people that do like the product, and then subtract from 100% to find the percent that don't like it. Equivalently, you can subtract 368 from 400 to get the number of people who did not like the product, and then use that number to compute the percent.

Using the second technique:

400 − 368 = 32 people who did not like the product. Then,

Percent of people who did not like the product $= \dfrac{32}{400} = 8\%$.

Answer #4: Ⓔ

Concept: • Solving inequalities

To find which of the above numbers is a possible value of P, we need to solve the inequality. Remember that solving inequalities is exactly the same as solving equations with one exception: whenever you multiply or divide by a negative number, you must change the direction of the inequality. Thus,

$4P + 7 \le 6P - 3$

$-2P \le -10$ Divide by −2, reverse the inequality sign

$P \ge 5$

5. Which of the following is the same as 0.0000083?

(A) 8.3×10^{-4}

(B) 8.3×10^{-5}

(C) 8.3×10^{-6}

(D) 8.3×10^{-7}

(E) 8.3×10^{-8}

8.3×10^{-6}

6. $\sqrt{18x^3} \cdot \sqrt{2x} =$

(A) $4x^2 \sqrt{5}$

(B) $6x \sqrt{x}$

(C) $3x^2 \sqrt{2}$

(D) $6x^2$

(E) $36x^2$

5. Ⓐ Ⓑ ● Ⓓ Ⓔ

6. Ⓐ Ⓑ Ⓒ ● Ⓔ

 DO YOUR FIGURING HERE

$\sqrt{18x^3} \cdot \sqrt{2x}$

$\sqrt{36x^4}$

$6x^2$

Answer #5:   Ⓒ

Concept: • Exponential notation, negative exponents

Definition: • $10^{-n} = \dfrac{1}{10^n}$

To solve this problem, simply remember that 10^{-n} is an indication that you should move the decimal point n places to the left. Since, if we start with 8.3, we need to move the decimal point 6 places to the left to obtain 0.0000083, the answer is 8.3×10^{-6}.

Answer #6:   Ⓓ

Concept: • Properties of square roots

Formula: • $\sqrt{m} \cdot \sqrt{n} = \sqrt{mn}$

To begin, you must remember the fundamental property of products of square roots:

$$\sqrt{m} \cdot \sqrt{n} = \sqrt{mn}$$

Using this property, we can see that

$$\sqrt{18x^3} \cdot \sqrt{2x} = \sqrt{18x^3 \cdot 2x} = \sqrt{36x^4} = 6x^2$$

7. The lines $x = 8$ and $y = 4$ intersect at the point

(A) $(4, 0)$
(B) $(0, 4)$
(C) $(8, 4)$
(D) $(4, 8)$
(E) $(4, 12)$

8. The sum of two numbers is 63, and one is 27 larger than the other. What is the smaller number?

(A) 16
(B) 18
(C) 26
(D) 31
(E) 45

7. (A) (B) (C) (D) (E)

8. (A) (B) (C) (D) (E)

 **DO YOUR FIGURING HERE**

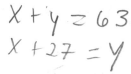

$$X + y = 63$$
$$X + 27 = y$$

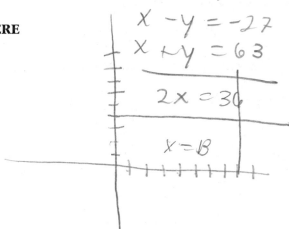

$$X - y = -27$$
$$X + y = 63$$
$$\overline{}$$
$$2x = 36$$
$$x = 18$$

Answer #7:   Ⓒ

Concept: • Ordered pairs, equations of horizontal and vertical lines

Formula: • $x = a$ for a vertical line (where a is the x-intercept)
$y = b$ for a horizontal line (where b is the y-intercept)

Definition: • x-intercept, y-intercept

The line $x = 8$ is the vertical line through the point (8, 0). Another way to think about this line is that it is the line that contains all of the points with x-coordinate 8. Similarly, the line $y = 4$ is the horizontal line through the point (0, 4). This line, then, is the line that contains all of the points with y-coordinate 4. Clearly, the only point that these two lines have in common is (8, 4).

Answer #8:   Ⓑ

Concept: • Solving algebraic word problems with two unknowns

The easiest way to solve this problem is to let $x =$ the unknown that we are trying to find, and then to express the other unknown in terms of x. Thus,

Let $x =$ the smaller number   Then,

$x + 27 =$ the larger number   since the larger number is 27 more than the smaller number

Next, use the fact that the two numbers add up to 63 to write an equation for x.

$$x + (x + 27) = 63$$

$$2x + 27 = 63$$

$$2x = 36$$

$$x = 18$$

9. Solve for x:

$$\frac{3x}{4} = \frac{4x - 1}{5} \left(5\right)$$

(A) −4
(B) −¼
(C) ¼
(D) 2
(E) 4

10. If John drives his car 8 miles in 12 minutes, what is his average speed in miles per hour?

(A) 30 mph
(B) 40 mph
(C) 44 mph
(D) 48 mph
(E) 52 mph

9. (A) (B) (C) (D) (E)

10. (A) (B) (C) (D) (E)

8 miles

 DO YOUR FIGURING HERE

$$\frac{(5)\,3x}{1 \cdot 4} = 4x - 1$$

$$(4)\,\frac{15x}{4} = 4x - 1\,(4)$$

$$15x = 16x - 4$$
$$-x = -4$$
$$x = 4$$

Answer #9: Ⓔ

Concept: • Solving proportions

Formula: • $\dfrac{a}{b} = \dfrac{c}{d}$ implies $a \times d = b \times c$

Definition: • Proportions

This equation has the same form as a proportion, and can be solved in the same way. Begin by cross multiplying.

$(3x)(5) = (4)(4x - 1)$ Now, multiply as indicated

$15x = 16x - 4$ Subtract $16x$ from both sides

$-x = -4$ Thus,

$x = 4$

Answer #10: Ⓑ

Concept: • Converting units of measure

Formula: • 60 minutes = 1 hour

To begin, we need to determine what fraction of an hour 12 minutes represents.

$$\frac{12 \text{ minutes}}{60 \text{ (min./hour)}} = \frac{12}{60} \text{ hours} = \frac{1}{5} \text{ hour}$$

Thus, John travels 8 miles in ⅕ of an hour.

$$\frac{8 \text{ miles}}{⅕ \text{ hour}} = 8 \times 5 \text{ mph} = 40 \text{ mph}$$

11. What is the least common denominator of $\dfrac{3}{8}$ and $\dfrac{5}{36}$?

(A) 36
(B) 48
(C) 72
(D) 108
(E) 144

12. $|6x - 3| > 9$ is the same as

(A) $x > 2$
(B) $x < -1$
(C) $x > -2$
(D) $-1 < x < 2$
(E) $x < -1$ or $x > 2$

---

11. (A) (B) ● (D) (E)

12. (A) (B) (C) (D) ●

✍ **DO YOUR FIGURING HERE**

$|6x - 3| > 9$

$6x - 3 > 9$
$\quad + 3 \quad + 3$

$6x - 3 < -9$
$\quad + 3 \quad + 3$

$\dfrac{6x}{6} < \dfrac{-6}{6}$

$x < -1$

Answer #11: Ⓒ

Definition: • Least common denominator

The least common denominator of 8 and 36 is the smallest number which can be evenly divided by both 8 and 36. While it is possible to deduce this from scratch, in a multiple-choice question, it is usually easier to just go through the answers, from smallest to biggest, until we find the first number that "works."

In this case, start with solution A. 36 is not divisible by 8, so we move to B. Since 48 is not divisible by 36, we move on to C. 72 *is* divisible by both 8 and 36, so it is the answer.

Answer #12: Ⓔ

Definition: • Absolute value
Concept: • Solving an absolute value equation

Absolute value equations and inequalities are a bit tricky. In this case, you must remember that there are two ways for $|6x - 3| > 9$. Of course, the inequality is true if $6x - 3 > 9$, but it is also true if $-(6x - 3) > 9$. Each of these inequalities must be solved separately. First of all, then,

$6x - 3 > 9$ Add 3 to both sides

$6x >$ 12 Divide by 6

$x > 2$ Thus, the inequality $|6x - 3| > 9$ is true for all $x > 2$.

Now, let's determine when the second inequality, $-(6x - 3) > 9$, is true.

$-(6x - 3) > 9$

$-6x + 3 > 9$ Subtract 3 from both sides

$-6x > 6$ Divide by -1. Remember to reverse the direction of the inequality

$x < -1$ Thus, the inequality $|6x - 3| > 9$ is also true for all $x < -1$.

Taking the solutions of the two inequalities together, we see that the inequality is true for all x such that either $x < -1$ or $x > 2$.

13. What is ½% of 1,500?

    (A) 0.075
    (B) 0.75
    (C) 7.5
    (D) 75
    (E) 750

14. Round 126,342 to the nearest ten thousand.

    (A) 130,000
    (B) 127,000
    (C) 126,000
    (D) 120,000
    (E) 100,000

13. Ⓐ Ⓑ Ⓒ Ⓓ Ⓔ

14. Ⓐ Ⓑ Ⓒ Ⓓ Ⓔ

 **DO YOUR FIGURING HERE**

Answer #13: Ⓒ

Concept: • Writing percents as decimals

Formula: • $A\% = \dfrac{A}{100}$

Begin by writing ½% with decimals; ½% = 0.5%. To change this percent to a pure decimal, simply divide by 100, which is the same as moving the decimal point two places to the left. Thus, $0.5\% = \dfrac{0.5\%}{100} = 0.005$.

Now, simply multiply 0.005 by 1,500.

$0.005 \times 1,500 = 7.5$

Answer #14: Ⓐ

Concept: • Rounding whole numbers

In the number 126,342, the digit in the ten thousands place is 2. All digits to the right of this digit will be replaced by 0s. Then, because the digit to the right of the 2 in the ten thousands place is greater than 5, we round the 2 up to a 3. This yields 130,000.

15. A square has the same area as a rectangle with length 27 and width 3. What is the perimeter of the square?

(A) 9
(B) 15
(C) 18
(D) 27
(E) 36

16. If $(x + 5)^2 = (x - 5)^2$, then $x =$

(A) −25
(B) −5
(C) 0
(D) 5
(E) 25

---

15. Ⓐ Ⓑ Ⓒ Ⓓ Ⓔ

16. Ⓐ Ⓑ Ⓒ Ⓓ Ⓔ

 DO YOUR FIGURING HERE

Answer #15: Ⓔ

Concept: • Areas and perimeters of squares and rectangles
Formula: • For a square, $A = s^2$ and $P = 4s$.
              For a rectangle, $A = LW$

The area of the rectangle would be $27 \times 3 = 81$. A square with the same area would have to have sides equal to $\sqrt{81} = 9$. Thus, the square is 9×9 and the perimeter is $9 \times 4 = 36$.

Answer #16: Ⓒ

Concepts: • Solving quadratic equations
               • Binomial products
Formulas: • $(a + b)^2 = a^2 + 2ab + b^2$
               • $(a - b)^2 = a^2 - 2ab + b^2$

To solve the equation, you must first perform the indicated multiplications

$$(x + 5)^2 = (x - 5)^2$$

$$(x + 5)(x + 5) = (x - 5)(x - 5)$$

$$x^2 + 2(5)x + 25 = x^2 - 2(5)x + 25$$

$x^2 + 10x + 25 = x^2 - 10x + 25$ Note that the x^2 and the 25 cancel out

$10x = -10x$ Divide by 10

$x = -x$ Add x to both sides

$2x = 0$ Divide by 2

$x = 0$

17.

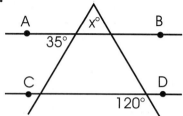

In the figure above, if AB is parallel to CD, then x =

(A) 35°
(B) 60°
(C) 75°
(D) 85°
(E) 120°

---

17. Ⓐ Ⓑ Ⓒ Ⓓ Ⓔ

 DO YOUR FIGURING HERE

Answer #17: Ⓓ

Concept: • The vertical angle theorem, alternate interior angle theorem

Definition: • Vertical angles, alternate interior angles

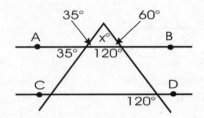

First of all, note that the angle in the lower left of the small triangle that sits on top of line AB has 35°, since it forms a vertical angle with the 35° angle below and to the left of it. Further, the angle in the lower right of the small triangle has 60°. This follows from the fact that it is supplementary to a 120° angle, whose measure we know because it is a corresponding angle to the 120° angle in the original figure. Finally, since every triangle contains 180°,

$$35° + 60° + x = 180°$$

$$95° + x = 180°$$

$$x = 85°$$

18. What is the value of ⅘ of
2.25 percent?

(A) $\dfrac{3}{250}$

(B) $\dfrac{1}{125}$

(C) $\dfrac{3}{500}$

(D) $\dfrac{9}{250}$

(E) $\dfrac{9}{500}$

---

18. Ⓐ Ⓑ Ⓒ Ⓓ Ⓔ

 DO YOUR FIGURING HERE

Answer #18: Ⓔ

Concept: • Fraction–decimal–percent equivalents

Answering this question requires the ability to manipulate fractions, decimals, and percents. There are several ways to proceed. One is to express both given numbers as decimals, and simply multiply them. Since $\frac{4}{5} = 0.8$ and $2.25\% = 0.0225$, we have

$$0.8 \times 0.0225 = 0.018.$$

This number must now be written as a fraction

$$0.018 = \frac{18}{1,000} = \frac{9}{500}$$

Another way to solve the problem is to leave $\frac{4}{5}$ as a fraction, write 2.25% as a fraction, and multiply

$$\frac{4}{5} \times \frac{2.25}{100} = \frac{4 \times 0.45}{100} = \frac{1.8}{100} = 0.018$$

19. If $3a = 7b$, then $14b - 6a =$

  (A) −8
  (B) 0
  (C) 3
  (D) 7
  (E) It cannot be determined

20. A rectangle has length L and width W. If the length of the rectangle is increased by 130%, and the width of the rectangle is decreased by 20%, what is the area of the new rectangle in terms of L and W?

  (A) .9LW
  (B) .96LW
  (C) 1.04LW
  (D) 1.1LW
  (E) 1.5LW

19. Ⓐ Ⓑ Ⓒ Ⓓ Ⓔ

20. Ⓐ Ⓑ Ⓒ Ⓓ Ⓔ

 DO YOUR FIGURING HERE

Answer #19: Ⓑ

Concept: • Manipulating equations with two unknowns

This is a rather tricky question. Many people who know that a single equation in two unknowns cannot be solved for a unique solution will choose E. However, note that it is possible to evaluate the given expression without actually finding a value for a and b.

To begin, rewrite $3a = 7b$ as $7b - 3a = 0$. Then, multiply both sides of this equation by 2.

$2(7b - 3a) = 2(0)$ Thus,

$14b - 6a = 0$

Answer #20: Ⓒ

Concept: • Finding a new value after a percent of change
Formula: • A = LW for a rectangle

The original rectangle has length L, width W, and area LW.

If the length is increased by 130%, it becomes 1.3L.

If the width is decreased by 20%, it becomes .8W.

Thus, the new area is $A_{new} = (1.3L)(0.8W) = 1.04LW$.

21. If N is an integer divisible by 4, which of the following is not necessarily an integer?

(A) $\dfrac{N}{8}$

(B) $\dfrac{N}{4}$

(C) $\dfrac{N}{2}$

(D) $N^2 + N$

(E) $N^2 + 1$

22. What is the value of sin 45° − cos 45° + tan 45°?

(A) −1

(B) $\dfrac{-\sqrt{2}}{2}$

(C) 0

(D) 1

(E) $\dfrac{\sqrt{2}}{2}$

---

21. Ⓐ Ⓑ Ⓒ Ⓓ Ⓔ

22. Ⓐ Ⓑ Ⓒ Ⓓ Ⓔ

 **DO YOUR FIGURING HERE**

Answer #21: Ⓐ

Concept: • Rules of divisibility
Definition: • Integer, divisible

First of all, note that both D and E can be eliminated, because if you square an integer and then add another integer to the result, you certainly end up with an integer. However, we need to consider the other choices more carefully, because when you divide an integer by another number, you may end up with a fraction. Note, however, that $\frac{N}{4}$ *is* an integer, since we were told that N is divisible by 4. And, of course, $\frac{N}{2}$ is also an integer, since any number divisible by 4 is divisible by 2. But, $\frac{N}{8}$ may *not* be an integer. A number that is divisible by 4 may not be divisible by 8. Consider, for example, the number 12. It is divisible by 4, but not by 8.

Answer #22: Ⓓ

Concept: • Evaluating the trigonometric functions for special angles

Formula: • $\sin 45° = \cos 45° = \frac{\sqrt{2}}{2}$, $\tan 45° = 1$

While in general the values of the trigonometric functions for particular angles need to be looked up in tables or evaluated with a scientific calculator, there are a few "special" angles for which it is possible to evaluate the trig functions using the rules of geometry. The values for these special angles should be memorized for use on the test. One of these angles is 45°, and it can be shown (and should be memorized) that $\sin 45° = \cos 45° = \frac{\sqrt{2}}{2}$, and $\tan 45° = 1$. Knowing this,

$$\sin 45° - \cos 45° + \tan 45° = \frac{\sqrt{2}}{2} - \frac{\sqrt{2}}{2} + 1 = 1.$$

23. The average of the annual salaries of five friends is $43,000. If the smallest of the five salaries is $25,000, which of the following could not be one of the remaining friends' salaries?

(A) $80,000
(B) $90,000
(C) $100,000
(D) $110,000
(E) $120,000

24. What is the number that is 80% of the distance between 9.20 and 9.80?

(A) 9.60
(B) 9.62
(C) 9.64
(D) 9.66
(E) 9.68

23. (A) (B) (C) (D) (E)

24. (A) (B) (C) (D) (E)

 **DO YOUR FIGURING HERE**

Answer #23: Ⓔ

Concept: • Averages

Formula: • $\dfrac{\text{The sum of all values}}{\text{The number of values}} = \text{Average}$

Before doing any work on the problem, it is wise to ask the question, "Why would there be any number that couldn't represent one of the salaries?" There are only two possible answers to this question: either a salary is so small that it would pull the average down so much that an end result of $43,000 would be impossible, or the salary is so large that it would pull the average up so much that an end result of $43,000 would be impossible. In this case, since all of the answers are greater than the average, the only possible option is that one of the numbers is too big. In this case, the largest answer, E, must be the one that is too big, since the others are smaller.

To look at this in a more quantitative way, suppose one of the salaries is, in fact, $120,000. The smallest salary is $25,000; let us say, for the purpose of discussion, that the other salaries are also $25,000 (that is to say, as small as possible). Then, the average would be: $\dfrac{(25{,}000 + 25{,}000 + 25{,}000 + 25{,}000 + 120{,}000)}{5} = 44{,}000$. Thus, if one of the salaries is $120,000, the smallest the average can be is $44,000, which is too big.

Answer #24: Ⓔ

Concept: • Decimal–percent equivalents

To begin, let us find the distance between 9.20 and 9.80

$9.80 - 9.20 = 0.60.$

Now, 80% of this distance = $0.80 \times 0.60 = 0.48$

Adding this amount to 9.20 gives us: $9.20 + 0.48 = 9.68$

25. Find the length of the line segment connecting the points with coordinates $(-1, 4)$ and $(-2, 1)$.

(A) $3\sqrt{2}$

(B) $2\sqrt{3}$

(C) $\sqrt{10}$

(D) $5\sqrt{2}$

(E) $2\sqrt{5}$

---

25. Ⓐ Ⓑ Ⓒ Ⓓ Ⓔ

 DO YOUR FIGURING HERE

Answer #25: Ⓒ

Concept: • Finding the distance between two points

Formula: • $\sqrt{(x_2 - x_1)^2 + (y_2 - y_1)^2} = d$

Definition: • The distance formula

The distance formula, which is really just the Pythagorean theorem, can be used to determine the distance between any two points. In this case, the points are $(-1, 4)$ and $(-2, 1)$. The formula tells us

$$d = \sqrt{(x_2 - x_1)^2 + (y_2 - y_1)^2}$$

$$= \sqrt{(-2 - (-1))^2 + (1 - 4)^2}$$

$$= \sqrt{(-2 + 1)^2 + (-3)^2}$$

$$= \sqrt{(-1)^2 + 9} = \sqrt{1 + 9} = \sqrt{10}$$

26. If $\dfrac{1}{x} + \dfrac{1}{2x} + \dfrac{1}{3x} = 11$, then $x =$

(A) ⅑
(B) ⅙
(C) ⅓
(D) ½
(E) 2

26.

 DO YOUR FIGURING HERE

Answer #26: Ⓑ

Concept: • Solving equations containing fractions
Definition: • Least common denominator

The safest way to handle an equation containing fractions is by getting rid of the fractions immediately. This can be accomplished by multiplying both sides of the equation by the LCD of the fractions.

In this case, the LCD is $6x$. Multiplying both sides by $6x$ yields:

$$6x\left(\frac{1}{x}\right) + 6x\left(\frac{1}{2x}\right) + 6x\left(\frac{1}{3x}\right) = (6x)\,11$$

$$6 + 3 + 2 = 66x$$

$$11 = 66x \quad \text{Divide by 66}$$

$$x = \frac{1}{6}$$

27. Brett Bayne still owes $\dfrac{5}{11}$ of a debt. If he makes a payment that represents $\dfrac{2}{7}$ of the original debt, what fractional part of the debt does he still owe?

(A) $\dfrac{5}{77}$

(B) $\dfrac{1}{11}$

(C) $\dfrac{1}{7}$

(D) $\dfrac{13}{77}$

(E) $\dfrac{15}{77}$

28. The dimensions of a rectangular den are 18 feet by 15 feet. How many square yards of tile are needed to cover the floor?

(A) 11 sq. yd.
(B) 30 sq. yd.
(C) 60 sq. yd.
(D) 90 sq. yd.
(E) 110 sq. yd.

---

27. Ⓐ Ⓑ Ⓒ Ⓓ Ⓔ

28. Ⓐ Ⓑ Ⓒ Ⓓ Ⓔ

 DO YOUR FIGURING HERE

Answer #27: Ⓓ

Concept: • Subtraction of fractions

All we need to do to solve this problem is to subtract the $\frac{2}{7}$ payment that he makes from the $\frac{5}{11}$ that he still owes.

$\frac{5}{11} - \frac{2}{7} =$ Change to a common denominator of 77

$\frac{35}{77} - \frac{22}{77} = \frac{13}{77}$.

Answer #28: Ⓑ

Concept: • Converting units of measure, area
Formula: • For a rectangle, A = LW

To start, be sure you read the problem carefully, so that you notice that the dimensions of the den are given in feet, while the answer asks for square yards.

When you are dealing with areas, it is usually less confusing to convert units right at the start. Thus, since there are 3 feet in every yard, express the measurements of the den as 6 yards by 5 yards. Then, the area is 6 × 5 = 30 square yards.

29. Express 0.0036 as a percent.

   (A) 0.000036%
   (B) 0.0036%
   (C) 0.36%
   (D) 3.6%
   (E) 36%

30. $(cot\ \alpha)\ (cos\ \alpha + tan\ \alpha\ sin\ \alpha)$ is equivalent to

   (A) $sin\ \alpha$
   (B) $cos\ \alpha$
   (C) $tan\ \alpha$
   (D) $\dfrac{1}{sin\ \alpha}$
   (E) $\dfrac{1}{cos\ \alpha}$

29. Ⓐ Ⓑ Ⓒ Ⓓ Ⓔ

30. Ⓐ Ⓑ Ⓒ Ⓓ Ⓔ

 DO YOUR FIGURING HERE

Answer #29: Ⓒ

Concept: • Changing decimals to percents

To express a decimal as a percent, you must multiply the decimal by 100 (that is, move the decimal point two places to the right) and append a percent sign. Thus,

0.0036 = 0.36%

Answer #30: Ⓓ

Concept: • Simplifying trigonometric expressions
Formula: • $\cos^2\alpha + \sin^2\alpha = 1$

A good way to begin is by expressing all of the functions here in terms of sines and cosines. Thus,

$$(\cot \alpha)(\cos \alpha + \tan \alpha \, \sin \alpha)$$

$$= \frac{\cos \alpha}{\sin \alpha}\left(\cos \alpha + \frac{\sin \alpha}{\cos \alpha} \times \sin \alpha\right)$$

$$= \frac{\cos \alpha}{\sin \alpha}\left(\cos \alpha + \frac{\sin^2 \alpha}{\cos \alpha}\right) \quad \text{Now, distribute}$$

$$= \frac{\cos^2\alpha}{\sin \alpha} + \sin \alpha \qquad \text{Rewrite with a common denominator}$$

$$= \frac{\cos^2\alpha}{\sin \alpha} + \frac{\sin^2 \alpha}{\sin \alpha} = \frac{\cos^2 \alpha + \sin^2 \alpha}{\sin \alpha} = \frac{1}{\sin \alpha}$$

31. A carpet installer estimates that he wastes 8.5% of his carpeting during the cutting and installation process. If, during a particular week, 20,200 square yards of carpeting were installed, approximately how many square yards were wasted?

    (A) 171.7
    (B) 184.8
    (C) 1,717
    (D) 1,848
    (E) 1,924

32. A particular copy machine can make 280 copies in 7 minutes. How many copies can it make in 4 minutes?

    (A) 40
    (B) 80
    (C) 120
    (D) 160
    (E) 200

31.　Ⓐ　Ⓑ　Ⓒ　Ⓓ　Ⓔ

32.　Ⓐ　Ⓑ　Ⓒ　Ⓓ　Ⓔ

 **DO YOUR FIGURING HERE**

Answer #31: Ⓒ

Concept: • Solving percent problems

Formula: • Part = percent × whole

In this percent problem, we have the *whole* (the total weekly carpet sales, 20,200 sq. yd.) and the *percent* (8.5%). We are looking for the *part* of the carpeting that is wasted. A *part* is always found by multiplying the *percent* times the *whole*. Thus,

$$20{,}200 \times 8.5\% = 20{,}200 \times 0.085 = 1{,}717$$

Answer #32: Ⓓ

Concept: • Solving proportions

Formula: • If $\dfrac{a}{b} = \dfrac{c}{d}$ then $ad = bc$

Definition: • Proportion

This problem can easily be solved by setting up a proportion relating copies to minutes. Let $x =$ the number of copies that can be made in 4 minutes.

$$\frac{280 \text{ copies}}{7 \text{ minutes}} = \frac{x \text{ copies}}{4 \text{ minutes}} \qquad \text{Cross multiply}$$

$$280 \times 4 = 7x$$

$$1{,}120 = 7x \qquad \text{Divide by 7}$$

$$x = 160$$

33. After a safety awareness program, the average number of accidents per year at a particular manufacturing company fell from 1,280 to 1,088. What was the percent of decrease in the number of accidents?

(A) 12%
(B) 15%
(C) 16%
(D) 18%
(E) 85%

34. A rectangular tank 20 inches by 8 inches by 4 inches is filled with a liquid. The liquid is to be transferred to smaller cubical tanks that are four inches on a side. How many such tanks would be needed to transfer all of the liquid?

(A) 6
(B) 7
(C) 8
(D) 10
(E) 12

33. Ⓐ Ⓑ Ⓒ Ⓓ Ⓔ

34. Ⓐ Ⓑ Ⓒ Ⓓ Ⓔ

 **DO YOUR FIGURING HERE**

Answer #33: Ⓑ

Concept: • Finding a percent of decrease

Formula: • Percent of decrease = $\dfrac{\text{Amount of change}}{\text{Original value}}$

Percent of decrease can be easily computed as the amount of change divided by the original value. In this problem, we know the original value is 1,280, and the new value is 1,088. Thus, the amount of change is 1,280 − 1,088 = 192. Then,

$$\text{Percent of decrease} = \frac{\text{Change}}{\text{Original}} = \frac{192}{1,280} = 0.15 = 15\%.$$

Answer #34: Ⓓ

Concept: • Volume of a rectangular solid, volume of a cube

Formula: • Volume = LWH in a rectangular solid,
Volume = s^3 in a cube

The tank holds 20 × 8 × 4 = 640 cubic inches of liquid. Each cubical tank holds 4 × 4 × 4 = 64 cubic inches of liquid. Since $^{640}\!/_{64}$ = 10, it is clear that we would need 10 tanks to hold all of the liquid.

35. The list price for a new swimming pool is $1,680. During an off-season sale, a discount of 40%, followed by an additional discount of 25%, is offered. What is the final sale price of the pool?

(A) $588
(B) $756
(C) $1,008
(D) $842
(E) $960

36. The angle of elevation from an observer at ground level to a vertically ascending rocket measures 55°. If the observer is located 5 miles from the lift-off point of the rocket, what is the altitude of the rocket?

(A) 5 sin 55°

(B) $\dfrac{5}{\sin 55°}$

(C) 5 cos 55°

(D) $\dfrac{5}{\cos 55°}$

(E) 5 tan 55°

35. (A) (B) (C) (D) (E)

36. (A) (B) (C) (D) (E)

 DO YOUR FIGURING HERE

Answer #35: Ⓑ

Concept: • Successive percents of discount

Formula: • Final price = original price × (100% − first percent of discount) × (100% − second percent of discount)

To begin, it is wise to recall the common error that many people make in solving successive discount problems. Frequently, the thinking is that a discount of 40% followed by a discount of 25% is equivalent to a discount of 65%. Thus, the final price would be 35% of the original.

The reason that this is incorrect is that the second discount is taken after the first discount, and is thus a markdown from an already reduced amount. The problem must be done in two steps. First, find the price after the 40% discount (which is 60% of the original price).

$1,680 × 60% = $1,008

Now, this price must be reduced by 25%.

$1,008 × 75% = $756

Answer #36: Ⓔ

Concept: • Solving right triangles

Formula: • $\tan a = \dfrac{\text{opposite}}{\text{adjacent}}$

The best way to begin is with a diagram of the situation:

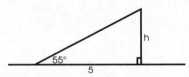

Let h = the altitude of the rocket. Then, since the tangent of an angle is equal to the opposite side divided by the adjacent, we have

$$\tan 55° = \frac{h}{5} \quad \text{or}$$

$$h = 5 \tan 55°$$

37. $(\sqrt{7} - \sqrt{3})^2 =$

(A) $10 - 2\sqrt{21}$

(B) $4 - \sqrt{7} - \sqrt{3}$

(C) $2 - \sqrt{7} - \sqrt{3}$

(D) 10

(E) 2

38. In New Jersey, the sales tax rate is 6% of sales. If the total cost of Paul's purchase, including the sales tax, is $84.80, what was the amount of the purchase before the sales tax was added?

(A) $78

(B) $79.71

(C) $80

(D) $80.48

(E) $82

37. Ⓐ Ⓑ Ⓒ Ⓓ Ⓔ

38. Ⓐ Ⓑ Ⓒ Ⓓ Ⓔ

 DO YOUR FIGURING HERE

Answer #37: Ⓐ

Concept: • Binomial products, properties of square roots

Formulas: • $(a - b)^2 = a^2 - 2ab + b^2$

$$\sqrt{m} \cdot \sqrt{n} = \sqrt{mn}$$

To solve this problem, simply perform the multiplication.

$$(\sqrt{7} - \sqrt{3})^2 = (\sqrt{7} - \sqrt{3})(\sqrt{7} - \sqrt{3})$$

$$= \sqrt{7}(\sqrt{7} - 2\sqrt{7}\sqrt{3} + \sqrt{3})\sqrt{3}$$

$$= 7 - 2\sqrt{21} + 3 = 10 - 2\sqrt{21}$$

Answer #38: Ⓒ

Concept: • Finding the original value before a percent of increase

Formula: • Original value $= \dfrac{\text{New value}}{100\% + \text{percent of increase}}$

Let's begin by looking at a very common mistake that people make when trying to solve problems such as this one.

Figuring that the price of the purchase with tax ($84.80) is 106% of the before tax price, people often simply take the $84.80 and reduce it by 6%. This would yield

$84.80 - (6\%)\,\$84.80 = (94\%)\,\$84.80 = \$79.71$. Thus, many people choose solution B. The reason this is incorrect is that the percentage given in the problem is a percentage of the before tax price, and *not* a percentage of the after tax price. Thus, it is incorrect to apply the percent to the $84.80.

Instead, think algebraically. Let P = the price before tax. Then, 106% of this price is $84.80.

$$106\% \times P = 84.80 \quad \text{Divide by } 106\%$$

$$P = \frac{84.80}{106\%} = \frac{84.80}{1.06} = \$80.$$

39. If sin α = ⁻³⁄₅, and cos α > 0,
   what is the value of cos α?

   (A) ³⁄₅
   (B) ⁴⁄₅
   (C) ¾
   (D) ⁴⁄₃
   (E) ⁵⁄₄

39. Ⓐ Ⓑ Ⓒ Ⓓ Ⓔ

  DO YOUR FIGURING HERE

Answer #39: Ⓑ

Concept: • Evaluating trigonometric functions
Formula: • $\cos^2\alpha + \sin^2\alpha = 1$

While there are a number of ways to answer this question (including using the formula $\cos^2\alpha + \sin^2\alpha = 1$ to solve for $\cos\alpha$), the quickest way to get the answer is as follows: since $\sin\alpha$ is defined as $\dfrac{\text{opposite}}{\text{hypotenuse}}$, we must have a triangle with one leg of length 3, and hypotenuse of length 5. Using the Pythagorean theorem, we can see the length of the other leg of the triangle (which must be the leg adjacent to α) is 4. Since $\cos\alpha$ is defined as $\dfrac{\text{adjacent}}{\text{hypotenuse}}$, and since we are given $\cos\alpha > 0$, we can see that $\cos\alpha = \frac{4}{5}$.

40.

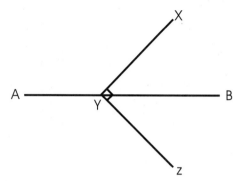

In the figure above, XY is
perpendicular to YZ. If angle
XYB measures 42°, what is
the measure of angle AYZ?

(A) 48°
(B) 126°
(C) 128°
(D) 132°
(E) 138°

40. (A) (B) (C) (D) (E)

  DO YOUR FIGURING HERE

Answer #40: Ⓓ

Formula: • If an angle has a°, the complement has 90 − a°, and the supplement has 180 − a°.

Definition: • Complements and supplements

Angle BYZ is the complement of XYB, and since XYB has 42°, the measure of BYZ is 90° − 42° = 48°. Then, angle AYZ is the supplement of angle BYZ, and since BYZ has 48°, angle AYZ has a measure of 180° − 48° = 132°.

41. If N is an integer, which of the following must be even?

(A) N + 1
(B) N + 2
(C) 2N + 6
(D) $\dfrac{N}{2}$
(E) 2N + 3

42. Chip buys a 32 oz. container of bromine concentrate for his spa. If each chemical treatment of the water in the spa requires 1⅓ oz. of bromine, how many full treatments does the container hold?

(A) 20
(B) 21
(C) 22
(D) 23
(E) 24

41. Ⓐ Ⓑ Ⓒ Ⓓ Ⓔ

42. Ⓐ Ⓑ Ⓒ Ⓓ Ⓔ

 DO YOUR FIGURING HERE

Answer #41: Ⓒ

Concept: • Odd and even numbers
Definition: • Integers

First of all, note that the problem asks which of the following *must* be even. This means that one of the answer choices above has to represent an even number regardless of the value for N. Now, let's consider the answer choices one at a time.

First of all, look at N + 1. If N is an even integer, then N + 1 is odd. As for the next choice, if N happens to be odd, then N + 2 is also odd. However, consider 2N + 6. Regardless of whether N is even or odd, 2N is even, and so is 2N + 6. So, it appears that C is always even.

Let's finish by considering the other choices. $\dfrac{N}{2}$ could be even or odd, depending on the value for N, and 2N + 3 is always odd.

Answer #42: Ⓔ

Concept: • Division with fractions

To solve the problem, we need to determine how many 1⅓ oz. treatments can be obtained from a 32 oz. bottle; that is, we need to find out how many times 1⅓ "goes into" 32.

$\dfrac{32}{1⅓}$ Express 1⅓ as ⁴⁄₃

$\dfrac{32}{⁴⁄₃}$ Invert the ⁴⁄₃ and multiply

32 × ¾ = 8 × 3 = 24.

43. The sides of a right triangle are 5, 12, and 13. Find the length of the altitude to the hypotenuse.

(A) $\dfrac{13}{60}$

(B) $\dfrac{12}{65}$

(C) $\dfrac{60}{13}$

(D) $\dfrac{65}{12}$

(E) 10

43. Ⓐ Ⓑ Ⓒ Ⓓ Ⓔ

 DO YOUR FIGURING HERE

Answer #43: ©

Concept: • The area of a triangle
Formula: • A = ½BH

To begin, make a sketch of the triangle.

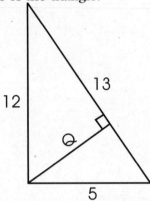

Now, this problem is very tricky if you do not realize that it is really an area question. Recall that the formula for the area of a triangle is A = ½BH, and that this formula holds regardless of the base and height used for the computation.

If we use the two legs of the triangle as the base and the height, we get an area of

A = ½BH = ½ × 12 × 5 = 30. Thus, the area of the triangle is 30.

Now, if we were to compute the area of the triangle using the hypotenuse as the base and the altitude to the hypotenuse (call it Q) as the height, we would have to get 30 as the answer. Thus,

A = 30 = ½BH = ½ × 13 × Q,   or

30 = ½ × 13 × Q   Multiply by 2

60 = 13Q   Divide by 13

$$Q = \frac{60}{13}$$

44. What is the slope of the line
described by the equation
$2x + 7y = 11$?

(A) $-\dfrac{7}{2}$

(B) $-\dfrac{2}{7}$

(C) $\dfrac{11}{7}$

(D) $-\dfrac{11}{7}$

(E) $-\dfrac{11}{2}$

44. Ⓐ Ⓑ Ⓒ Ⓓ Ⓔ

 DO YOUR FIGURING HERE

Answer #44: Ⓑ

Concept: • Slope–intercept form of a line

Formula: • $y = mx + b$

Perhaps the quickest way to find the slope of a given line is to rewrite the equation in the slope-intercept form, $y = mx + b$, where m is the slope and b is the y-intercept.

$2x + 7y = 11$ Subtract $2x$ from both sides

$7y = -2x + 11$ Divide by 7

$y = -\dfrac{2}{7}x + \dfrac{11}{7}$

It can be seen that the slope of the line is $-\dfrac{2}{7}$.

45. If a particular commemorative coin is to contain 8.32 grams of gold, find the number of coins that can be produced from 221 grams of gold.

(A) 25
(B) 26
(C) 27
(D) 28
(E) 30

46. *XY* is the diameter of a circle. If the coordinates of *X* are (3, 9), and the coordinates of *Y* are (9, 3), what are the coordinates of the center of the circle?

(A) (3, 3)
(B) (12, 12)
(C) (6, 12)
(D) (12, 6)
(E) (6, 6)

45. (A) (B) (C) (D) (E)

46. (A) (B) (C) (D) (E)

 DO YOUR FIGURING HERE

Answer #45: Ⓑ

Concept: • Division with decimals

Solving this problem simply involves finding out how many "8.32s" we can get out of 221. To determine this, we simply need to divide.

$$\frac{221}{8.32} = 26.6. \quad \text{Thus, we have enough gold to make 26 coins.}$$

Be careful not to round up your answer. We need to have a full 8.32 grams for every coin.

Answer #46: Ⓔ

Concept: • The midpoint formula

Formula: • Midpoint $= \left(\dfrac{x_1 + x_2}{2}, \dfrac{y_1 + y_2}{2}\right)$

The center of a circle is the midpoint of the endpoints of any diameter.

To solve this problem, all we need to do is find the midpoint of (3, 9) and (9, 3).

Midpoint =

$$\left(\frac{x_1 + x_2}{2}, \frac{y_1 + y_2}{2}\right) = \left(\frac{3 + 9}{2}, \frac{9 + 3}{2}\right) = \left(\frac{12}{2}, \frac{12}{2}\right) = (6, 6).$$

47. In triangle PQR, PQ = QR. If angle P = $3x - 20$, and angle Q = $2x + 28$, find the number of degrees in angle R.

   (A) 36
   (B) 48
   (C) 52
   (D) 72
   (E) 104

48. An automotive dealership claims that its brand of tires will last for 30% more miles than a competitor's brand. If the dealer's brand of tires gives 58,500 miles of service, how many miles would be expected from the competitor's brand?

   (A) 40,950
   (B) 42,000
   (C) 45,000
   (D) 46,000
   (E) 46,950

47. Ⓐ Ⓑ Ⓒ Ⓓ Ⓔ

48. Ⓐ Ⓑ Ⓒ Ⓓ Ⓔ

 DO YOUR FIGURING HERE

Answer #47: Ⓒ

Concept: • The base angles in an isosceles triangle are equal
Definition: • Isosceles triangle

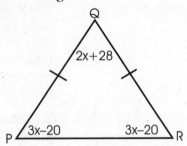

In an isosceles triangle, if PQ = QR, then angle P and angle R are congruent. Thus, angle R = $3x - 20$. Since the triangle must contain 180°,

$$(3x - 20) + (3x - 20) + (2x + 28) = 180$$

$$8x - 12 = 180$$

$$8x = 192$$

$$x = 24$$

If $x = 24$, then $3x - 20 = 3 \times 24 - 20 = 52$.

Answer #48: Ⓒ

Concept: • Finding the original value before a percent of increase

Formula: • Original value $= \dfrac{\text{New value}}{100\% + \text{Percent of increase}}$

Let C = the mileage expected from the competitor's brand

Then, C + 30% (C) = 58,500   or

130% (C) = 58,500   Divide by 130%

$$C = \frac{58,500}{130\%} = \frac{58,500}{1.3} = 45,000$$

49. In a triangle, the angles are in a ratio of 3 : 4 : 5. What is the number of degrees in the largest angle of the triangle?

(A) 60°
(B) 75°
(C) 80°
(D) 85°
(E) 90°

50. If x is negative and y is positive, which of the following will *always* be positive?

(A) $x + y$

(B) $\dfrac{x}{y}$

(C) xy
(D) $x - y$
(E) $y - x$

49. Ⓐ Ⓑ Ⓒ Ⓓ Ⓔ

50. Ⓐ Ⓑ Ⓒ Ⓓ Ⓔ

 DO YOUR FIGURING HERE

Answer #49: Ⓑ

Concept: • Ratios, 180° in a triangle

The easiest way to solve this problem is to picture the ratio of $3 : 4 : 5$ as follows: the 180° of the triangle are divided up into $3 + 4 + 5 = 12$ parts. Each of the parts, then, consists of $\dfrac{180}{12} = 15°$. The smallest angle in the triangle contains 3 of the 15° parts, the middle angle contains 4 of the 15° parts, and the largest contains 5 of the 15° parts. The largest angle, thus, has $5 \times 15° = 75°$.

Answer #50: Ⓔ

Concept: • The rules of sign

The problem asks us to determine which of the expressions is *always* positive. Let's look at them one at a time and think about whether we can say anything about their signs or not.

First of all, $x + y$ could be either negative or positive, depending on the relative magnitudes of x and y. Next, $\dfrac{x}{y}$ and xy are actually always negative, since we are multiplying or dividing a negative and a positive number. Then, note that $x - y$ is also negative, since a negative minus a positive is always negative. However, the final choice *is* always positive. A positive number minus a negative number is the same as two positives added together, and is, thus, positive.

If you are stuck on this problem, consider selecting values for x and y, and then plugging them in to the answer choices. This process should make the correct solution fairly obvious.

51. How many feet are there in y yards, f feet, and i inches?

(A) $y / 3 + f + 12i$
(B) $3y + f + i /12$
(C) $3y + f + 12i$
(D) $y/3 + f + 12/i$
(E) $3y + f + 4i$

52. If v videotapes cost d dollars, what is the cost in dollars of q videotapes?

(A) $\dfrac{dq}{v}$

(B) $\dfrac{d}{qv}$

(C) $\dfrac{q}{dv}$

(D) $\dfrac{dv}{q}$

(E) $\dfrac{qv}{d}$

51. (A) (B) (C) (D) (E)

52. (A) (B) (C) (D) (E)

 DO YOUR FIGURING HERE

Answer #51: Ⓑ

Concept: • Conversion of units of measure

In y yards there are $3y$ feet, since there are 3 feet in a yard.

In i inches, there are $\dfrac{i}{12}$ feet, since each foot has 12 inches.

Thus, in y yards, f feet, and i inches, there are $3y + f + \dfrac{i}{12}$ feet.

Answer #52: Ⓐ

Concept: • Solving proportions

Formula: • If $\dfrac{a}{b} = \dfrac{c}{d}$ then $ad = bc$

Definition: • Proportion

This problem can best be solved by setting up a proportion. Let $x =$ the cost in dollars of q videotapes. Then, form two ratios, and set them equal:

$$\frac{v \text{ videotapes}}{d \text{ dollars}} = \frac{q \text{ videotapes}}{x \text{ dollars}} \qquad \text{Cross Multiply}$$

$vx = dq$ Divide by v,

$$x = \frac{dq}{v}$$

53. Brian spent ⅓ of his Christmas gift money on a present for his mother, and ⅗ of what was left on a present for his father. If after these purchases he had $16 left, how much money did he begin with?

(A) $45
(B) $60
(C) $90
(D) $120
(E) $240

54. If $A = -3$, $B = -2$, and $C = 5$, what is the value of $\dfrac{(A-B)(B-C)}{A-C}$?

(A) $-\dfrac{35}{8}$

(B) $-\dfrac{7}{8}$

(C) $-\dfrac{3}{8}$

(D) $\dfrac{3}{8}$

(E) $\dfrac{7}{8}$

---

53. Ⓐ Ⓑ Ⓒ Ⓓ Ⓔ

54. Ⓐ Ⓑ Ⓒ Ⓓ Ⓔ

 DO YOUR FIGURING HERE

Answer #53: Ⓑ

Concept: • Solving arithmetic word problems
Formula: • Fraction × whole = part

This is another question that must be read very carefully. For starters, we know Brian spent ⅓ of his money on his mother. This leaves him ⅔ of his money.

Brian now spends ⅗ *of what was left* on his father. This means that he spent ⅗ of the remaining ⅔ on his father. Be careful that you do not accidentally compute ⅗ of the ⅓ that he spent on his mother.

Now, ⅗ of ⅔ = ⅗ × ⅔ = ⅖ of his money that Brian spends on his father.

He now has spent ⅓ + ⅖ = ⁵⁄₁₅ + ⁶⁄₁₅ = ¹¹⁄₁₅. Thus, Brian has 1 − ¹¹⁄₁₅ = ⁴⁄₁₅ left to spend. Since we are told that Brian has $16 left, we know that ⁴⁄₁₅ of Brian's money is $16. We can now find out how much money Brian started with by using a little algebra.

Let M = The amount of money Brian started with. Then,

⁴⁄₁₅ M = 16   Multiply both sides by ¹⁵⁄₄

M = 16 × ¹⁵⁄₄ = 60. Therefore, Brian started with $60.

Answer #54: Ⓑ

Concept: • The rules of sign, the order of operations

To solve this problem, simply plug in the numbers and carefully follow the rules of sign and order of operations.

$$\frac{(A-B)(B-C)}{A-C} = \frac{(-3-(-2))((-2)-5)}{-3-5}$$

$$= \frac{(-3+2)(-2-5)}{-3-5} = \frac{-1 \times -7}{-8} = \frac{7}{-8} = -\frac{7}{8}.$$

55. If $3x - 2y = 7$, and
$-2x + 5y = 12$, what is the
value of $x + 3y$?

(A) 5
(B) 12
(C) 19
(D) 36
(E) 39

56. If $9x^2 - 4y^2 = 0$ and
$3x - 2y = 7$, what is the
value of $3x + 2y$?

(A) -8
(B) -5
(C) 0
(D) 5
(E) 8

55. Ⓐ Ⓑ Ⓒ Ⓓ Ⓔ

56. Ⓐ Ⓑ Ⓒ Ⓓ Ⓔ

 DO YOUR FIGURING HERE

Answer #55: Ⓒ

Concept: • Combining linear equations in two unknowns

There are two ways to solve this problem. The obvious way would be to use either the addition method or the substitution method to find the common solution (x, y), and then plug into the expression $x + 3y$. However, there is a much quicker "trick" that can be used to solve the problem.

Note that you are not asked to actually find x or y, but instead the combination $x + 3y$. Sometimes, the problem is actually set up to enable you to find $x + 3y$ by combining the given equations directly. In this problem, start by lining up the two equations:

$$3x - 2y = 7$$

$$-2x + 5y = 12$$

Now, note that if you add the two equations together, the left sides to the left sides and the right sides to the right sides, you immediately get $x + 3y = 19$.

This trick will certainly not always work, but it is worth a try whenever you are asked to find the value of a combination containing x and y, instead of x and y individually.

Answer #56: Ⓒ

Concept: • Factoring the difference of two squares
Formula: • $a^2 - b^2 = (a - b)(a + b)$

Note that $9x^2 - 4y^2$ is the difference of two perfect squares, and can thus be factored by the above formula.

$$9x^2 - 4y^2 = (3x - 2y)(3x + 2y) = 0$$

Now, since the product $(3x - 2y)(3x + 2y)$ is equal to 0, it must be true that either one factor or the other is, in fact, equal to 0. However, we are told that $3x - 2y = 7$. Thus, it must be true that $3x + 2y = 0$.

57. According to a survey, 38% of the residents of Tonawanda read the morning paper, and 72% read the evening paper. If 13% of the residents read no paper at all, what percent of the residents read both the morning and evening paper?

   (A) 17%
   (B) 19%
   (C) 23%
   (D) 25%
   (E) 28%

57. Ⓐ Ⓑ Ⓒ Ⓓ Ⓔ

DO YOUR FIGURING HERE

Answer #57: Ⓒ

Concept: • Solving set problems
Definition: • Venn Diagrams

This problem can be solved by drawing a Venn Diagram and labeling the appropriate regions. In the diagram, the leftmost circle represents people that read the morning paper, and the rightmost circle represents readers of the evening paper. The overlapping area, then, represents the people who read both. The area outside of the circle can be used to represent the people who do not read either paper.

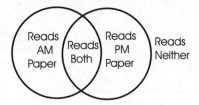

Now, begin by labeling the overlapping region x%, since this is the unknown value. Then, it must be the case that $(38 - x)$% of the people read the morning paper and $(72 - x)$% read the evening paper.

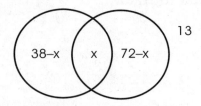

Since each person either reads both papers, neither paper, or one paper or the other, it must be true that:

$(38 - x)$% + $(72 - x)$% + x% + 13% = 100%.   Then,

123% − x% = 100%

x% = 23%

58. At State University this semester, 24% of the total enrollment are married. If there are 420 married students, what is the total enrollment?

(A) 1,680
(B) 1,720
(C) 1,740
(D) 1,745
(E) 1,750

---

58. Ⓐ Ⓑ Ⓒ Ⓓ Ⓔ

 DO YOUR FIGURING HERE

Answer #58: Ⓔ

Concept: • Solving percent problems

Formula: • $\text{Whole} = \dfrac{\text{Part}}{\text{Percent}}$

Recall that every percent problem involves three quantities, a *whole* (in this case the total enrollment), a *part* (the number of married students), and a *percent* (in this problem, 24%). Thus, in this problem, we know the part and the percent and we are looking for the whole. The whole is equal to the part divided by the percent. Thus,

$$\text{Total Enrollment} = \frac{420}{24\%} = \frac{420}{0.24} = 1{,}750.$$

59.   If $\dfrac{x + y}{z - y} = 7$, and

$\dfrac{z - y}{x - y} = 12$, what is the value of $\dfrac{x + y}{x - y}$?

(A) $\dfrac{7}{12}$

(B) $\dfrac{12}{7}$

(C) 5

(D) 19

(E) 84

---

59. Ⓐ   Ⓑ   Ⓒ   Ⓓ   Ⓔ

 DO YOUR FIGURING HERE

Answer #59: (E)

Concept: • Algebraic manipulation of fractions

This is a very tricky question. You can spend a lot of time trying to solve for x, y, and z, and probably end up nowhere. But note, once again, that you are never asked to find the values of x, y, and z, but actually the value of the expression $\dfrac{x + y}{x - y}$. Also note that the two expressions whose values you are given contain the expressions $(x + y)$ and $(x - y)$. The question is, is there some way to combine the two given expressions in such a way as to make them equal to $\dfrac{x + y}{x - y}$?

If you play around with the expressions a little bit, you will see that if you multiply them together, you will get exactly what you want.

$$\left[\frac{x + y}{z - y}\right]\left[\frac{z - y}{x - y}\right] = \frac{x + y}{x - y}$$

Thus, the solution to the problem is simply 7 x 12 = 84.

60. A square is inscribed in a circle of radius 4. What is the area of the square?

(A) 16
(B) 24
(C) 32
(D) 48
(E) 64

60. Ⓐ Ⓑ Ⓒ Ⓓ Ⓔ

 DO YOUR FIGURING HERE

Answer #60: ⓒ

Concept: • 45 – 45 – 90 Triangles
Formula: • Leg = hypotenuse/$\sqrt{2}$

As always, begin by making a sketch.

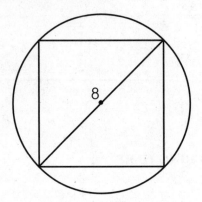

The key thing to note is that the diameter of the circle, which is 8, is also the diagonal of the square. Thus, the square has a diagonal of 8.

Note that two legs of the square, along with the diagonal, form a right triangle. Since the two legs of the square are the same, we could use the Pythagorean theorem to determine them. However, it is a lot quicker to simply notice that the triangle is a 45 – 45 – 90 triangle, and in such a triangle you can determine the length of the legs by dividing the hypotenuse by $\sqrt{2}$. Thus, the length of a leg = $\dfrac{8}{\sqrt{2}}$ = $4\sqrt{2}$.

The area of the square is $4\sqrt{2} \times 4\sqrt{2} = 16 \times 2 = 32$.

CONCEPT TO PROBLEM INDEX

Each problem in this book tests one or two math concepts. This index lists the 120 problems in this book, by the concepts each question tests. As you work on these two ACT tests, refer to this index when you have a problem with a question. When you have answered all of the test questions, you can then refer to this index and quickly identify those skill areas that need additional review. Then, using the index, once again, go back to those specific questions and reread the solutions. (Note: The numbers listed for each concept refer to the test number, problem number, and page number, which appears in parentheses.)

Arithmetic

Algebra

155

Exponents and Square Roots	1-3 (5), 1-5 (7), 1-32 (43), 1-36 (47), 1-38 (49), 1-40 (51), 2-5 (87), 2-6 (87), 2-37 (123)
Functions	1-44 (57)
Products and Factoring	1-4 (5), 2-16 (97), 2-56 (145)
Signed Numbers	1-38 (49), 2-50 (139), 2-54 (143)
Solving Equations	1-3 (5), 1-5 (7), 1-8 (11), 1-20 (27), 1-37 (49), 1-39 (51), 1-42 (55), 1-46 (61), 2-9 (91), 2-16 (97), 2-19 (103), 2-23 (107), 2-26 (111), 2-55 (145)
Solving Inequalities	1-33 (45), 2-4 (85), 2-12 (93)
Word Problems	1-18 (23), 1-26 (35), 1-50 (67), 2-8 (89)

Coordinate Geometry

Distance and Midpoint Formulas	2-25 (109), 2-46 (135)
Equations of Circles	1-14 (19)
Equations of Lines	1-9 (11), 1-13 (17), 2-7 (89)
Ordered Pairs	1-9 (11)
Slopes	1-11 (15), 1-12 (17), 2-44 (133)

Plane Geometry

Circle Geometry	1-29 (39), 1-34 (45), 1-45 (59)
Measures of Angles	1-22 (29), 2-40 (127)
Squares and Rectangles	1-45 (59), 1-49 (65), 2-15 (97), 2-20 (103), 2-28 (113)
Triangle Geometry	1-7 (9), 1-49 (65), 1-53 (71), 1-57 (77), 2-17 (99), 2-43 (131), 2-47 (137), 2-49 (139), 2-60 (153)
Volume	1-59 (79), 2-34 (119)

Trigonometry

Evaluating Trigonometry Functions	1-24 (33), 1-43 (57), 2-22 (105), 2-39 (125)
Identities	1-10 (13), 2-30 (115)
Word Problems	1-60 (79), 2-36 (121)

Other

Probability	1-35 (47)
Set Theory and Notation	1-41 (53), 2-57 (147)

ADDITIONAL WORK SPACE

ADDITIONAL WORK SPACE

ADDITIONAL WORK SPACE

ADDITIONAL WORK SPACE

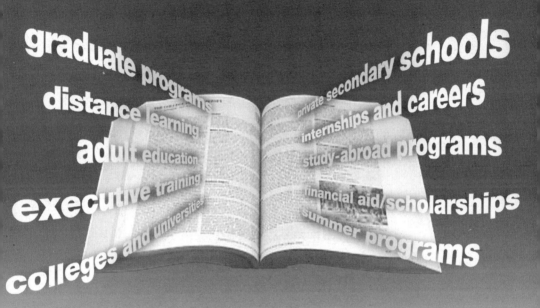